T5-ANW-109

WOMANHOOD

Raoul Mortley

Womanhood

The feminine in
Ancient Hellenism,
Gnosticism,
Christianity,
and Islam.

Delacroix
Press

First published in Sydney by DELACROIX
Copyright 1981, Raoul Mortley. All rights reserved.
Enquiries: 66 Evans St.,
           Rozelle,
           NSW 2039,
           Australia.

BL
458
.M77
1981

ISBN 0 9594165 0 1

Printed by Southwood Press, Marrickville 2204, Australia

Cover
Woman's theatre mask, Hellenistic style from Roman
Imperial period, published by courtesy of the Selcuk Museum
Directorate, Turkey. Cover designed by Sandy Aureli.

Contents

Plates

Note on references
All references have been included in the text in abbreviated
form, and are cited in full at the end of each chapter.

INTRODUCTION

Feminism has implications for historical research, since it provides a focus for the historian's attention. Historical writing is largely a matter of focus, and the feminist movement has drawn attention to a class of society whose conditions of life have been infrequently and incompletely explored. In recent years several useful books have appeared in the general area of the study of women in antiquity, and the present author seeks to contribute by examining the religious and philosophical influences on the place allocated to women within the life of society. To this end the idea of woman, and the place of woman, is studied in relation to the religion of Isis, Hellenistic Judaism, early Christianity, Gnostic Christianity, later orthodox Christianity, and Islam.

Philo, a Jewish writer from Alexandria, provides a unique insight into the Hellenistic understanding of womanhood because he uses the metaphor of male and female continually, in order to make his theological and philosophical points. In his writing, woman is identified with body and the senses, and therefore with changeability and instability, whereas man symbolises mind and the loftier intellectual pursuits of the spirit. No clearer source than this can be found for the medieval portrayal of man as *spiritus* and woman as *anima* (see Joan M. Ferrante, *Woman as Image in Medieval Literature,* N.Y. 1975). On the other hand, the religion of Isis provides a female deity and a point of identification for woman, and a certain measure of responsibility for women in the organisation of the cult, though how significant this is is open to question.

The discussion of Gnosticism and other contemporary movements such as Pythagoreanism brings to the fore the interest in bisexuality as a symbol of completeness and harmony, which manifested itself in late antiquity through an interest in defining God, or at least those beings superior to ordinary humans, as bisexual. This idea is juxtaposed with the Hellenistic interest in hermaphrodites, reflected in the hermaphroditic sculptures which were typical of the period. In our own time, some writers have been inclined to question that metaphorical language which describes God in masculine terms, and the late Greek interest in bisexual imagery needs to be contrasted with this. This androgynous motif is closely related with the Greek understanding of love (*eros*) and desire, since these are conditions which are thought to be the symptoms of incompleteness and loss: the androgyne is considered to be a total being.

The interpretation by the ancient Christian church of Paul's claim that 'in Christ there is neither male nor female' is examined in order to determine whether it was understood in a social sense, as endorsing some idea of equality or unity between men and women, and an examination of the citation of this verse by the Christian fathers is carried out in an attempt to arrive at a definite statement of how the ancient Church viewed this Pauline principle. Again, in our time, some have sought to use this passage in order to endorse the demands of women for the right to be ordained to the priesthood in various branches of the Christian church. It will be found that Patristic Christian writers did not see Paul's statement as having any significance for the role of women in ecclesiastical organisation.

Lastly, the transition to Islam will be examined, with particular attention to the teaching of the Koran on the nature of women and marriage. The Arab practice of polygamy is often made the particular culpable responsibility of Muhammad, but it is argued that he endeavoured to improve the situation of women in a reformist manner, though of course he was far from denouncing the phenomenon. Some reference is made to present-day marriage legislation in Islamic countries, in particular to the Iranian civil code under the recently deposed Shah, and its section on the status of women. Particular thanks are due to two Iranian friends for assistance on this issue, and who should remain nameless in the present situation. As the saying goes, the author alone is to be held responsible for any shortcomings in what follows. Particular thanks are expressed to Robbie Kenna for her capable typing of the manuscript, and for some observations of her own.

R.J.M.

Chapter One

Hellenism

Some feminist literature has taken to the field of historical research, and an odd example of this is provided by Merlin Stone's *The Paradise Papers* with its millenialist views on the advantages of the primacy of female deities. This book combines the visionary with some useful historical material: it claims in general that in the Prehistoric period the gods were understood as being female. At a certain point the human race turned towards maleness and patriarchal religion, and this occurred at the outbreak of the Western era, with the advent of Zeus, Jesus and eventually Muhammad. The book is itself an historical curio, providing as it does an example of contemporary romantic feminism: 'In the worship of the female deity, sex was Her gift to humanity. It was sacred and holy. She was the Goddess of Sexual Love and Procreation. But in the religions of today we find an almost totally reversed attitude. Sex, especially non-marital sex, is considered to be somewhat naughty, dirty, even sinful' (170).

The prehistoric freedom of the libido is said to be the direct result of the dominance of female deities, and there is some suggestion of a golden age in the period thus described. The advent of the classical period saw a new and threatening male dominance, and the rise of Christianity served to compound this disaster with its acceptance and dissemination of the myth of Eve, which provided a typology of womanhood which was malicious and repressive. This is a serious point and will be examined later. Yet it should be noted that the myth belongs to that alleged golden age, and there are also problems of time-scale in the discussion of the Egyptian goddess Isis: it is true that under the reign of Isis women in Egypt, the Greek East and Italy found a deity with which they could identify, but this is part of the classical world, and in no way prehistoric. The material taken from Diodorus and Strabo does not help with the general hypothesis of an earlier and different era dominated by female deities.

This book is scarcely a serious contribution to historical enquiry, but it does exemplify some widespread tendencies. There is the notion that the deity, if represented as feminine, will help engender humane and civilising values. The male religions come later to replace these goddesses with hard, moralistic systems destructive of both love and life. There is simply no evidence that the sex of the deity has this social correlate: in fact it is certainly the case that in the religion of Isis an austere moralism was practised, which was every bit the equal of that practised by its Christian rival. (The question of the moral standards of the followers of Isis is well discussed by Sharon Kelly Heyob, in *The Cult of Isis among Women in the Graeco-Roman World*.) It is almost impossible to correlate the sex of the principal deity with the value-systems of his/her followers, and the simple proposition that the female goddess produces female values (whatever these are) must surely be questionable. It glides over the whole issue of the relation of myth to society, and it could even be argued, a la Feuerbach, that myth is a *result* of the social process. On this view the sex of the gods would be an effect rather than a cause, but one would have to look astonishingly hard at the data to be able to specify the nature of the relationship, and we must be sceptical about 'solutions' to these issues. This question will come up again when Gnosticism is discussed: in this context Elaine Pagels argues more plausibly for 'a correlation between religious theory and social practice' (*The Gnostic Gospels* 60).

In fact the late classical period is not at all the male preserve in matters of religion that it is claimed to be. It manifests a considerable variety of religions, and there coexist religions for men (Mithras) and religions for women (Isis), religions with male deities (Judaism), religions with female deities, and religions with androgynous deities. These last may be found in Gnosticism and Neopythagoreanism, and some interest in bisexuality may also be found in Hellenistic Judaism. That this era is not at all the age of the exclusively male religion is clear enough from Book XI of Apuleius' *Metamorphoses,* where Isis is identified with countless local deities, all of them female, and all of them bearing witness to flourishing female deities on the local level. The period in question is one of intense variety, and what follows will seek to illustrate the different currents of Hellenism which stood side by side.

Plutarch

The plays of Menander give an insight into the bourgeois way of life of the Hellenistic Greek world, and the behaviour and problems of womanhood feature prominently in them. Problems of finance, frequent discussions of appropriate dowries, incongruities of class background, and the other logistic problems of the bourgeois life make up the stuff of these plays. As has been noted by Elaine Fantham, two female types predominate among the female characters in the plays, namely the established wife and the hetaera, or courtesan, who is often bad-tempered, petulant and extravagant (72). Greek actors used masks, and though a large number of different masks for female characters were available for use, Fantham argues that these two types emerge particularly clearly. The way of life enjoyed by ordinary couples is what emerges most clearly from the plays of Menander, and this provides an excellent backdrop to the social context iń which Plutarch writes.

Bourgeois living is replete with prescribed limits and rules of behaviour, and its drama and tension arises out of minor contradictions between these, and out of the general problem of living a rule-bound existence. A whiff of this way of life comes from several of Plutarch's minor works in the category known as his *Moralia*. In his *Advice to Bride and Groom,* the reader feels strongly the sense of constraints imposed by this kind of life, constraints which seem to turn on behavioural rules which are trivial, and which themselves turn on distinctions which are reinforced by nothing else than the desire to have such distinctions. The example of the European bourgeoisie will seem much closer to this than that of the New World, which is not quite as constrained by this excess of delicatesse.

Plutarch quotes Solon's advice that the bride should eat a quince (*Moralia* 138D) before getting into bed, and a similar passage in 279F seems to indicate that this was a remedy against halitosis, and if so one wonders why this affliction was thought less offensive in the male than the female. Married women are advised to make themselves conspicuous when they are with their husbands: it is at this time that they should be at their most visible, but if their husbands are absent they should remain at home, keeping themselves concealed (139C). Women are considered naturally extravagant, and will vigorously maintain such tendencies if husbands try forcibly to contain them. If however, an appeal is made on the basis of reason women do respond and practise moderation. Plutarch quotes the story that Cato expelled a man from the Senate because he had kissed his wife in front of his daughter, and while he finds it a little severe, he does extend the anecdote into a rule that husbands and wives should not bring their personal animosities and disagreements into the open, conducting their battles before outsiders. This precept, directed against public fault-finding with one's spouse, will be recognised as being designed to reinforce the privacy of marriage and the primacy of the couple as the basic module out of which society is built.

Plutarch, whilst taking a very firm line about the modesty which becomes a wife, is completely indulgent about possible sexual adventures on the part of the husband (140B). The wife should be prepared to accept this, since the fact that he wishes to share his debauchery with another rather than her, enhances her position. It shows that she is respected. A wife should not derive her substance from her wealth, social status or physical attractiveness, but from her ability to captivate her husband by conversation, temperament and companionship (141A). Female wiles find approval with Plutarch (142A-B): a woman must be prepared to joke with her husband, and should not be too fearful of appearing audacious. Like a poet or an orator, whose diction is finely tuned in order to avoid vulgarity though at the same time managing to persuade, she must deploy all her talents to educate him into liking that which is both honourable and pleasant (142B). A woman takes her identity from her husband, since she should speak either to him or through him, and should not be aggrieved if her utterance takes on a finer sound through the tongue of another. The Aphrodite of Elea was sculpted by Pheidias with one foot on a tortoise, which for Plutarch symbolises the idea that a woman should keep at home and keep silence (142D).

A woman's husband should be her guide and mentor (145C), and an interest in philosophy and geometry will keep her from untoward conduct, or trivial pursuits such as dancing, or an excessive interest in astrology. There is a distinct danger that a woman's mind, if left untended by these husbandly attentions will develop badly, and produce evil infections like certain uterine outgrowths which Plutarch describes (145D).

The *Consolation to his Wife,* which he wrote to her following the death of their daughter, has a strong flavour of sharing and partnership, but is remarkable for the fact that its emphasis falls almost entirely on the problem of containing one's emotions.

Emotional restraint is an ethical value which no doubt stems from the Stoic idea of *apatheia,* a word which we should translate by the English 'impassivity', and which refers to the deliberate effort to foster emotional continence. Plutarch involves this standard for himself as well as his wife, but there appears to be a suggestion that excessive display of temperament is more of a female failing. He commends his wife (608F) for the manner in which she conducted the funeral in his absence: she did not put on mourning garb, there was no sumptuous display, and everything was done in silence. Plutarch regards the temptation towards lamentation to be a considerable one, and speaks with distaste of the habit of wailing and beating one's breast. He notes that excessive laughter and expression of joy is also to be avoided, and this too illustrates the influence of the Stoic ideal of impassivity, which existed to discourage all extreme expressions of emotion, of whatever kind. (This is of course a very different ethic from that obtaining in our own post-Freudian culture, in which the free and unobstructed expression of emotion is thought to produce mental health, and in which any attitude involving inhibition, suppression or repression is thought to produce mental and physical diseases of the direst kind.) Plutarch considers that the trappings of mourning, such as short-cropped hair and the presence of wailing women, only serve to render the grief more acute, and contribute to general and long-lasting emotional disarray.

Plutarch's wife must have been a model of Stoic impassivity. While other women were putting scented unguent on their hair

(609B) and wearing purple, and in time of mourning cutting their hair short and dyeing their clothes black, she was known for her plain dress and sobriety of living. Her simplicity was well known among the townsfolk and among Plutarch's philosophical friends, and her self-possession was such that many of those who gathered at the house after the death of the child wondered if the report of her death were not a mere rumour. Such is the ideal held out to womanhood: austerity and rigid control of the emotions, and the latter was held to be a particularly difficult problem for women. The situation is not very different with Philo, and in this author the idea that women are particularly emotionally unstable will emerge more clearly.

Philo

Philo, a Greek-influenced scholar and statesman of Alexandria in the first century BC, has a great deal to say about women as metaphors for social or psychological states, but little to say about their actual social status. On one of the rare occasions when he actually gives an insight into the social history of the period, Philo claims, in accordance with a Deuteronomy precept, that whatever else may be tolerable in a market-place, a woman must not grasp hold of the genitalia of her opponent. Not even the fact that she may be defending her husband should absolve her, and as a punishment it is proposed that her hand be cut off, this being intended to have a deterrent effect on would-be genital-snatchers. One may observe here that a specifically female form of self-defence against men is being curtailed. Philo also applauds the managers of gymnasia who disallow the attendance of women, since athletics was a male pursuit, practised naked. 'Each sex should avert its eyes from the nakedness of the other, thus complying with the decrees of nature' (*Special Laws* III. 176).

Philo is always ready to attribute differences in role and personality between men and women to 'nature'. In the same way as much modern discussion turns on the relative contribution of heredity and environment in the constitution of the personality, the Greeks had long debated the function of nature as against custom (*nomos*) in determining ideas and actions. Philo thus had available to him the possibility of seeing sex roles as determined by custom or convention, but as we would expect, fails to show any interest in this alternative. He invariably attributes what he sees as the female character and status to 'nature'. Sons, for example, are to inherit the goods of their parents, and daughters only where there are no sons. This 'natural' precedence which men have over women ought to be reflected in their legal relationships (*Special Laws* II.124). Dowries are necessary, however, to protect the interests of women, and it is interesting to note that where no dowries are left, daughters should share equally with males. The needs of destitute girls are to be superintended by a civil authority, who must also arrange for a suitable marriage to take place. This authority apparently had to arrange for a dowry, but marriage within the same deme or tribe is specified as being more desirable, since in this case the funds or goods involved would not fall into other hands.

In the *Sacrifices of Abel and Cain* (101) the distribution of sex roles is said to be a form of *arete* (virtue/function), meaning that certain attributes constitute the specific function of the individual sexes. Men and women cannot debate with each other over what is proper to each category, and they cannot, even by long practice, expect to annul the discrimination laid down by nature. Here Philo clearly repudiates the possibility that the difference in behaviour between the sexes is a matter of 'custom', and rigidly polarises their roles. Girls behave 'daintily', whereas it is characteristic of youths to work hard: exchanging these characteristics will lead to punishment (*Moses* 1.54). The dominance of the male, and his completeness, leads Philo to suggest that the male is akin to the abstract notion of casual activity. The female, being incomplete and passive, is akin to the caused: she awaits stimulus and direction (*Special Laws* I.200). In the same work (I.105) the advantage of virgins is said to be that they are easily influenced, and thus may be attracted to virtue. Like a sheet of wax which has been levelled out, they await an imprint which will determine their character. By contrast, the male nature is more active than that of the woman; he is prone to action, and this is why he undertakes responsibility for taking a woman out of her parent's home, and setting her up in his own (*Questions and Answers on Genesis* I.29). The male espouses a younger wife, since Woman is younger than Man, being created second: thus it is contrary to nature to espouse a woman who has passed beyond her prime. Affairs of state are the business of a man, while household management is that of a woman.

Much of the above material is based on what Philo considers to be 'nature', and that which is natural is of course understood in relation to the Genesis account of the origins of nature. His continued reference to the inferiority of the female is not mere assertion on his part, as Baer suggests (41), but is based on his belief that this is part of the natural order as constituted by God in his act of creation. More will be said on the cosmological basis of his ethical attitudes, but it can be noted here that even the Law, far from being an arbitrary set of norms, is said to be 'consequent on nature' (*Special Laws* II.129). This emphasis on nature leads to an emphasis on the typology of male and female as written into the cosmic order by the creation process. Eve is not simply an image or analogy for womanhood: she is the prototype of the natural female.

The Eve model is thus of crucial importance, not only in Philo, but also in the Patristic writers (i.e. the Church Fathers), and in the New Testament. The fact that she was created second in time has been alluded to above, but the subsequent events leading to the Fall do more to determine the future of womanhood. When tempted by the Serpent, which Philo understands allegorically as Pleasure, she falls victim to her own lack of steadfastness and strength (*On the Creation* 156). Pleasure directs its attack to the female first, since she represents the senses, whereas the man represents mind. Pleasure, the Satanic principle, seeks to excite the senses in order that they may influence and captivate the mind: we all have male and female within us, being composed of both mind and senses, and are therefore susceptible to these temptations. As the woman tempts the man, so the senses attempt to distract mind by the delight of various savours and sounds, the fragrance of perfumes and the sight of colours and shapes. Woman thus acts as a procurer for the Serpent, her function being to ensnare the lover (mind) for the principle of pleasure. Eve is identified with sense-perception in the *Allegorical Interpretations* (III.56), and the fact that two separate recipients were found for the Mind and the Senses is interpreted to mean that sense is not always subservient to or under the control of Mind.

It was because this was her nature that the Serpent brought his attack to bear on the woman, his appeal being to the senses, in the hope that this more susceptible element might be willing to influence and captivate the mind. Reason would thus lose its dominance, which process Philo compares to becoming subject, enslaved, alien and mortal. The Fall brings certain consequences for women; whilst toil and technical skill are henceforth required of the man, the woman must bear children in painful labour, and assume responsibility for the upbringing of her children in all circumstances. Next, she loses her freedom and must now accept the mastery of her husband (*On Creation* 167).

The view of woman as sensual leads Philo to elaborate extrapolations on this theme, allowing him to weave an entire ethical and psychological pattern (drawn from his own experience of women) into the Genesis allegory. Throughout the portrait of woman which emerges, maleness is presented as an ideal state often contrasted with womanhood, or womanishness. The true-born child of virtue, the bearer of joy, is to be a son, free from all female *pathos,* or sensitivity to affections (*On the Change of Names* 261): the idealisation of masculinity will reappear in relation to Philo's view of spiritual growth, which he compares to achieving maleness. The view of woman as Sense-perception leads Philo to all kinds of extravagances on the theme of female sensuality. Her irrationality, and capacity for fear, sorrow, pleasure and desire renders her desperately weak and changeable (*Questions and Answers on Genesis* IV.15). The question of why Rebeccah leapt from her camel at the sight of Isaac, is answered by reference to the submissive nature of woman, and her need for self-abasement before male virtue (*Questions and Answers* IV.142). The male is more complete and more dominant than the female, and is closer to 'causal activity' (*Special Laws* I.200).

Philo's elaborate description of Pleasure is apparently based on an image of contemporary female coquetry:

> Her gait has a looseness bred of excessive indulgence and luxury; the voluptuous movement of her eyes is a bait to draw the spirits of the young; her gaze is bold and shameless, her neck held high, her posture unnatural to her; she grins and giggles. Her hair in extraordinary and complicated plaits, she has lines drawn under her eyes, and painted eyebrows; she constantly indulges in warm baths, and has contrived her flushed colouring... (*The Sacrifices of Abel and Cain* 21).

In close relation with her are all sorts of vices, such as faithlessness, flattery, deceit and injustice: these all assail the Mind, with Pleasure standing in their midst like a chorus-leader.

Elsewhere (*On Husbandry* 72) Philo takes the analogy of two horses, Desire and High Spirit, to elucidate the sexual differences: the latter prances, his neck high, seeking freedom 'as a male', whereas the former lacks freedom, is servile, mischievous, and eats one out of house and home, 'for she is female'. Similarly, women are more prone to jealousy (*Special Laws* I.108). Femininity is by nature flaccid: it will yield easily to deception, whereas the intellectual power of the man will enable him to dispel falsehood (*Questions and Answers* I.33). This is the general outline of Philo's picture of women, and with this in mind we are able to commiserate with Lot in that he had fathered daughters only, and was unable to rear any male, or perfect, offspring (*On Drunkenness* 164).

The passages reported immediately above reveal a rather concrete image of womanhood, and provide the elements for what one suspects would be Philo's portrait of contemporary Alexandrian woman. There is little philosophical theory here, but much use of what seems to be Philo's own experience of womanhood for the purpose of developing a principle of femininity. It is possible however, to discover in Philo a number of reflections on the womanly state which are not so contemptuously dismissive as the portrait thus pieced together. There is a place for women in Philo's ethics: there are traces of a positive assessment of their role, which by no stretch of the imagination could be called egalitarian, but which envisages an essential function for women in the construction of society. The positive assessment is also prescriptive and restrictive in character, and is highly paternalistic, but in the interests of historical accuracy it is important that it should be formulated, not least because a superficial reading of Philo's works may create the impression that he regards woman as nothing more than a blight on the cosmos and society, her usefulness being approximately equivalent to that of a burden.

The understanding of the procreation process is always an important barometer for the rise and fall of the regard in which women are held. It has been noted that man is the active, or causal, element in male/female relationships, and this datum reemerges in the discussion of procreation. Whereas woman mistakenly believes herself to be the cause of generation, her function is in fact passive. She 'undergoes' rather than acts: the man alone is the cause of that which comes into being (*On Drunkenness* 73). It is clear that being born of the womb is a second-rate manner of achieving one's existence: the first Woman was created by the act of a male God, and thus enjoyed an initially pure existence. The world's beauty lies partly in the fact that it was begotten by the Father alone: it was motherless and came into existence through means other than the womb. Thus it did not take its origin from corruption, nor is it subject to corruption (*Moses* II.210). In another passage however (*The Eternity of the World* 98) it is admitted that the womb is a necessary part of procreation, since the seed by itself is incapable of producing fullness. Just as the earth nourishes and sustains the seed planted in it, so the womb provides essential nourishment for the embryo. Some physiological precision is given to this in *On the Creation* 131, where it is said that the watery element is that which binds the earth together. This watery substance is 'the part of the earth which gives birth to all things' (132), and it brings seeds to birth in the case of the earth. The watery substance is present in the female menstrual cycle, and Philo quotes unnamed 'physicists' on behalf of the idea that the foetus is composed of it. There is an elaborate development here of the idea of the earth mother, and Plato is quoted with approval as saying that the earth does not imitate women, but women the earth. Both are impregnated with life-giving and sustaining moisture. Philo leaves aside the question concerning the specific mechanism of conception, and the relative importance of the male seed and the female 'wet substance', though his language seems to imply that the female has a fairly crucial role in the conception process. She is more than a mere 'place' for the seed to grow.

Woman also has a definite social role. The mother is identified with instruction (*paideia*), and her task is training offspring in those established customs which are universally accepted (*On Drunkenness* 81). Philo is establishing a dichotomy of his own between the educative role of the father and that of the mother, using that of Proverbs 1.8 as a basis. The father is equated with 'right reason', whose role is to instruct the young in the knowledge of the 'Father of All'. This does not merely involve the knowledge of God, but the philosophical principle that correct knowledge begins from a proper understanding of the nature and source of the whole universe. Such a holistic approach to knowledge, whereby God is best considered and known from an overall cosmological standpoint, will be found among some of the Greek Christian writers, and it is Philo's thought that the superior rationality of the male equips him to instruct the young in the understanding of the world and its Maker, particularly since the reason which he shares is the primary principle of cosmology. By contrast, the woman's role is that of conveying an understanding of custom and convention. Later (*On Drunkenness* 84) the man is said to lay down 'laws' (*nomous*), the woman precepts (*thesmous*) for her offspring. This distinction is recapitulated in 95, where the father is said to lay down the commands of 'right reason', and the mother the observances of instruction. In 164 the alleged female sensitivity to custom is shown to have a dangerous aspect: Lot's wife, who was turned to stone, is interpreted allegorically as 'habit' (*sunetheia*). Her nature is said to be inimical to truth; she tends to lag behind, over-attached to familiar and traditional objects. This tendency, one may guess, is the risk inherent in the mother's proclivity for the understanding of convention: the father's reason leads him to the essence of things, whereas the mother's sensuality attunes her to the contingent norms of social organisation, but does not provide her with the critical apparatus necessary for evaluating them.

Certain elements in the equation of woman with the senses suggest a positive evaluation of her function. The *Allegorical Interpretations* III.56 gives an interesting view of the Fall. The Woman is of course sense-perception, and is to a certain extent condemned since the senses may range freely despite the efforts of mind to control them. Yet in 58 it is noted that the mind would have been incapable of perceiving colour, sound, hearing, odours, and taste without the gift of sense-perception. Without this mind could not enter into contact with the world. In 222 it is argued that mind must hold sway over sense-perception, since it is right that the superior should rule the inferior; in this way priorities are established. The 'female' contribution is nevertheless an essential function. Once again, though, it is an

Isis and her son Harpocrates (Karganis, a Coptic Fresco, 3rd. century A.D.). A demonstration of the Isis/Mary Syncretism — a non-christian Madonna with child.

ambivalent one. In 61 a clear distinction is drawn between the Woman's tempting of Adam, and her own temptation by the Serpent. Eve merely gave, whereas the Serpent beguiled. Thus sense-perception presents to the mind what is white, as white, or what is hot, as hot: pleasure however falsifies and adds glamour, as the courtesan paints her face, to the object which it presents to the mind. (This distinction between the two temptations will be found in the Christian Fathers, and is usually made in order to diminish Eve's responsibility in the matter.) The creation of sense-perception may allow the possibility of evil, but in its best form, sense-perception is simply an ethically neutral part of the ordinary human knowing apparatus. Woman is identified with perception and the life of the body, but the misuse of this is the principle of pleasure, and is reserved for separate identification (*On Husbandry* 97).

Thus one may conclude that for Philo the image of womanhood is not entirely negative, there being a certain neutral area where woman is simply accepted as a contributing part of reality and as having a necessary function. Of course the whole question of the status of this function and its relation to the hierarchy of functions, has yet to be asked, but it can be noted that there is in Philo no unilateral judgment of woman as evil. It is more a question of what limits he ascribes to the female function, and how these affect her status in relation to the male.

The problem to be considered here is Philo's frequent use of the concept of virginity. What immediately excites the curiosity of course, is that there is no corresponding idea of the value of male virginity; nor is there any suggestion that this state might be of benefit to both men and women. Why then is the suppression of sexuality of more importance for women than men?

It seems that virginity is closely connected with some kind of aesthetic ideal; Leah sometimes veils her face, and sits by the road with the appearance of a harlot in the hope that the curiosity of passers-by may be stimulated. Leah for Philo represents virtue, and her wish is that the inquiring mind may unravel her true beauty — her uncorrupted, undefiled and genuinely virginal beauty (*The Preliminary Studies* 124). Virginity and beauty are related because true beauty appertains to the higher level of intelligent activity: the High Priest is married to a virgin, which means that the seed he sows results in virginal and undefiled thoughts. He is the father of holy *logoi,* or rational ideas (*On Dreams* 185). The realm of intelligent activity is more beautiful because it escapes the degeneration of multiplicity and change. Rebeccah, we are told, was not only a virgin, but also a beautiful virgin. Virtue alone of created things is beautiful and good, and free from dissembling and defilement. Leah is above the passions, yet this estrangement from humanity also results in closeness to God; she brings to birth beautiful ideas, worthy of their Father. It is noteworthy that some women pass from womanhood to virginity: in other words it is possible to move from the corruptible and passion-bound state, to union with the incorruptible (*The Posterity and Exile of Cain* 133). Naturally the genuine virgin is in a better position, being entirely innocent and unfamiliar with corruption. She is more naturally attracted to virtue, and for this reason the High Priest must marry neither a widow nor a divorcee (*The Special Laws* I.105). Virginity is the state of not being subject to the passions (*Questions and Answers* IV.95).

There is an important link between virginity and maleness, since it seems that the former is a kind of female attempt to reproduce the greater spirituality of the male character. In the *Worse Attacks the Better* 28 it is argued that the passions are feminine by nature, and the ethical goal must be to pursue 'the masculine characteristics of the noble affections'. *On Drunkenness* 59 states that the 'customs of women are still among us; we are as yet unable to cleanse overselves of them, and flee to the dwellings of men'. But the identification of spiritual growth with becoming male is nowhere so clearly stated as in *Questions and Answers on Exodus* (I.8), where we are told that progress is giving up the female gender by changing into the male, since the latter is active, rational and intelligent and the female is passive and matter-bound.

Philo gives no clear anatomy of the female psychology which might show precisely how the female mind is more subject to matter than the male, and conversely how the male manages to escape so successfully the consequences of being tied to his body. In vain do we look for a precise statement of the relation of the intelligence, the soul and the body in either males or females, such as we might expect from Aristotle or Plotinus. This is probably the result of Philo's method of commentary and allegory, which effectively prevents him from lengthy discursive treatments of philosophical themes, but it means that we do not see quite how the female intellect and the female soul experience a greater degree of subjection to the female body than does the male to his own. Nevertheless the result is clear: only by the strenuous effort of virginity (that is, a greater degree of suppression of the flesh than is called for from the male) can the female hope to compete with her counterpart on the moral and spiritual level. She must become asexual.

Now the first Man, in Philo's understanding of *Genesis,* was either asexual or bisexual. R. A. Baer (20-44) has done much to elucidate the problem of understanding exactly what Philo is saying here. The complications arise from the fact that Philo seems to have many 'men' in mind, and wishes to foist various stages of creation on the narrative of *Genesis* 1 and 2. The main passages are *On the Creation* 76, 134, and 151: in the first of these it is said that the first man created is a genus, whose individual members have not yet taken shape. However the genus contains within itself the species of male and female. Yet 134 adds a nuance: man at this stage is neither male (*arren*) nor female (*thelu*). One must conclude that the earlier passage refers to the potential of the genus: when it has divided itself out, its species will be seen to be two-fold, male and female. But in strict terms the original Adam is neither. This state would in my view be better referred to as asexuality rather than bisexuality or androgyny, since sex is simply the drive which seeks to reunite the species once they have been separated (see 152). The notion of sex is irrelevant to Man, at the stage of the genus where no division has occurred. Thus originally Man is asexual, but in 134 another stage occurs, tied in Philo's interpretation to *Genesis* 2.7: 'God formed man by taking clay from the earth, and breathed into his face the breath of life'. This second Genesis reference to the creation of man enables Philo to see a second stage: that of the separating out of the genus into its species. The man now formed is an object of sense-perception, he has perceivable qualities (a characteristic of matter), he consists of body and soul, is mortal, and is man or woman. This must mean that the two material species have made their appearance, and 151 is devoted to explaining their mutual relations now that this differentiation has occurred. The function of love is to bring together the divided halves; it establishes in them a desire for unity, and for reproducing their likeness. It also produces sexual desire, which is the source of all sorts of wrong-doing and violation of the law. Then follows the analysis of the tree of life, and the work of the serpent.

Philo's anthropology clearly envisages a descent through various stages of which the last is the most degenerate, and consists in the differentiation of Man into male and female. This is the stage of matter, desire and the passions, and therefore of things which militate against the spirit. The ideal stage of manhood is the first stage, where there is no sexuality and no sexual differentiation. Virginity is an attempt to retrieve this asexuality, an attempt to return from the realm of the material to the realm of mind and ideas. It is an attempt to evade the consequences of the sexual differentiation which resulted from the last stage of creation. It represents an heroic effort to wrest oneself out of the material existence of the present to achieve the true spirituality of earliest Man. (Clearly asexuality could be a male ideal for the same reasons, but it is not until the growth of the monastic ideal in later Christianity that this option will be taken up: it would appear that in Philo, the male has a natural asexuality. Perhaps, alternatively, he never raises the questions of male abstinence in order to avoid prescribing norms for male behaviour.)

While it has been conceded that Philo is prepared to make some positive statements about the nature and role of woman, for example that she represents the necessary faculty of perception, or that she is able to teach her offspring the norms of conventional society, it is clear that these views imply subordination of female to male. The female function is necessary and valid, but always in a low position in the hierarchy of functions: the image of man as mind tells the whole story, since the possession of this faculty places him in a position of dominance. Mind is the faculty which brings him into a closer relationship with divinity, and which enables him to pass judgment on what he senses. Mind also allows him to see the essence of things, whereas woman's capacity is that of understanding mere convention. Such an understanding can be overturned at any point by man's superior insight into the world.

Philo's anthropology has two major strands. Man, as mind,

knows the world: the definition of male and female has strong roots in cosmology. Man is attuned to reason (*logos*), the principle on which the world is constructed: this allies him with the permanent and the stable. Woman's greater affinity with matter places her in the category of the unstable, the changing and the corruptible. The polarisation of male and female thus follows the lines of an ontological division familiar since Plato, and axiomatic in all thought influenced by him: the distinction between Being and Becoming. As noted earlier, Philo wishes to insert the male/female differentiation into nature itself, and denies that it is a cultural matter. The Law 'follows the course (*akolouthia*) of nature' (*Special Laws* II.129); the term here is a technical one, and has been analysed by the present author in relation to Clement of Alexandria, a later writer. The 'sequence of nature' is the sequence of natural relationships which occur in the world, and has a reflection in the natural sequence of ideas: it is something akin to the idea of the laws of nature in the strong sense, and suggests that there is a natural and necessary sequence of causal relationships. For Clement this 'sequence of nature' results in natural theology, which is a kind of parallel reflection of cosmological truth and which therefore possesses the authority of actual reality. For Philo, the Law follows the sequence of nature: it is not therefore an arbitrary set of norms, an ethical code created by divine fiat, but is the embodiment of certain principles enshrined in cosmological reality. Thus the Philonic definition of male/female relationships is not contingent or changeable; it is rooted in nature itself.

The second main source of Philo's anthropology is his interpretation of Eve. Philo takes the Genesis story as archetypal: it is the subject of allegorical interpretation, but cannot be dismissed as merely mythical.

> Now these are no mythical fabrications, such as the poets and sophists rejoice over, but patterns and models, calling for allegorical interpretation on the basis of the exposition of hidden meanings.

> (*On the Creation* 157)

The Genesis story for Philo is neither myth nor scientific history (in fact Philo has no sense of history whatever), but a symbolic way of referring to cosmic reality. This places a burden of interpretation on the reader, and in this way Philo draws far more material out of the Adam/Eve story than he would have had he regarded the story as simply historical. The view that it is symbolic provides a licence for extravagances of interpretation.

For this reason it cannot be said that the Adam/Eve story completely determines Philo's views of womanhood. The way in which he uses it is his own responsibility, and reflects preoccupations which spring from a general group of social pressures of which he is a part. It is of course true that the Genesis story leads to certain irreducible conclusions about the status of women, but Philo adds to these considerably: the principal feature of this burden is the absolute polarisation of male and female. Just as the Pythagoreans drew up tables of cosmic opposites, such as night and day, so Philo (who may be influenced by Pythagoreanism) here puts man and woman into separate categories, thereby bringing about a complete differentiation. The list of male and female qualities reads like a table of opposites: man as mind, woman as the senses; man as active, woman as passive; man as strong, woman as changeable. It is this tendency which causes Philo to caricature male/female relationships, since there can be no shared ground. The drive towards differentiation means an excessively rigid division in the definition of male and female. For these reasons it must be concluded that *Genesis* 1 and 2 does not determine Philo's views so much as the current interpretation of these chapters, and into this interpretation are built contemporary philosophical pre-occupations as well as the socially determined views of woman-hood which obtained at the time. The Genesis story is the pole around which the issue of womanhood turns, but each author has his own way of dealing with it.

The Cult of Isis

Sarah Pomeroy (217) emphasises the religion of Isis as a significant force for the emancipation of women, and contrasts it with traditional Roman religion, claiming that Isis 'did stand for the equality of women', and wondering how the lot of women in Western culture might have evolved if the 'religion of Isis had been triumphant' (226). There is a clearly implied comparison here with the religion which was in fact triumphant, Christianity, and the status of women in these respective cults must accordingly be examined. It must be noted on Isis' behalf that she does not benefit from the same exhaustive scrutiny as does her competitor, probably because her followers are now considerably fewer in number than those of Christ, and the question or ordination to the priesthood in her service is no longer an issue which causes anguish to large sections of the community. Nevertheless for feminism the relative assessment of the two movements is crucial, and the fact is, as Pomeroy (following Malaise's evidence) indicates, that there were female priests in the religion of Isis. In respect of the diffusion of the Isis cult in Italy, Malaise (127) cites twenty-six inscriptions referring to priests (the Latin term is *sacerdos*), of which six refer to women: he notes that this term always refers to a function within the religion of Isis, except in one case where the *sacerdos* concerned is also a priest of Sarapis (the inscriptions are collected by M. Malaise, *Inventaire préliminaire*...). This author also notes that one inscription refers to the priest as *publicus*, from which he plausibly draws the implication of a privately organised cult elsewhere, not recognised by the State. The priests of Isis are not only both male and female, but their social background also shows great variety. Since their names reveal different racial backgrounds, it would appear that in Isis, there is neither Jew nor Greek, bond nor free, male nor female. Malaise regards the entry of women into the priesthood as a late phenomenon, occuring in Italy under the Roman Empire, and regards it as evidence of Egyptianisation. The tendency to equate increased feminine influence with increased Egyptian influence must have been common in antiquity also: the power, capacity and dominance of the Egyptian queens was an exceptional fact in late antiquity, and their culmination in the extraordinary career of Cleopatra VII must have made a mark on the thought of many an observer. Diodorus even attributes the dominance of women over men in ordinary Egyptian society to the influence of the religion of Isis (I.27), taking a simplistic view of religion as a social cause. An Oxyrhynchus papyrus (11.1380.214-16) however lauds the power of Isis, claiming that 'she made the power of women equal to that of men'. Her priests must have conveyed a dramatically ascetic impression, with their shaven heads, and faces, their white linen robes, and their shoes of papyrus; the priestesses cultivated an appearance like that of representations of the goddess, sometimes with a fringed cloak draped over their shoulders. Both priests and priestesses were subject to dietary restrictions. The fact that there is a *mimesis* of the appearance of the goddess in that of her priestess is striking, since it would seem to bring her close in power and authority to Isis herself.

The fact that there were priestesses in the Isis cult is not in itself a significant fact: it acquires significance from the fact that in one of the competing religions, namely Christianity, women were not permitted to become priests. The word *sacerdos* has a fairly general usage in Latin, and can also apply to the vestal virgins, for example, although no one would claim that the right of a woman to become a vestal virgin is a sign of emancipation: the Greek equivalent of *sacerdos* is probably *hiereus,* and this is the word which must be pursued in connection with both Christianity and the Isis cult. In other words the issue is: how important is the priest(ess) in the hierarchy of the Isis cult itself, and secondly does the priesthood have the same kind of authority in both religions? On the first count Apuleius informs us of a high priest (*summus sacerdos-archiereus*), a priest and a scribe (*Metamorphoses* XI.16), but this applies to Cenchreae and it would be imprudent to assume that exactly the same hierarchical arrangements existed elsewhere. There is, however, evidence of some form of general hierarchy, and Malaise (citing W. Otto) concludes on the basis of both literary and epigraphical evidence that a class of priests superior to what might be called 'deacons' should be postulated. But it is quite probable that the word priest(ess) could refer to a variety of lower functions, and even the apparently menial function of carrying the container bearing ritual objects or books in the sacred procession, that is, the function of *canephoros* ('basket-carrier').

Slightly after the appearance of Malaise's work, Françoise Dunand's three volume study of the religion of Isis in the eastern Mediterranean basin appeared (Brill, 1973), and her third volume is devoted to clergy and ritual in the Isiac sactuaries. Dunand notes the increased participation of women in the cult in the period of the Roman Empire (167), but is on the whole inclined to minimise the importance of women in the hierarchy of the cult, alluding to what she considers to be the surprisingly small number of priestesses in a cult which offered a patron goddess for women, and leaving open the question of whether they were able to 'undertake cultic acts' (III.163). Despite her vagueness over the definition of 'cultic acts', one must in general agree that the mere mention of a *hiereia* (priestess) in a Greek inscription (see Dunand III.166-7), or of a feminine *sacerdos* in an Italian inscription is not sufficient. It may be suspected that some scholars seize on the use of these words in the context of the Isis cult in order to show that she permitted women to be ordained to the priesthood, whereas the followers of Jesus did not, but in fact the notion of 'priesthood' in the Isis cult must be treated as a completely separate issue. The problem lies in the lack of information about the precise boundaries of the Isis priesthood, and therefore about the degree to which woman may have had religious power over its organisation. In Greece, the *canephoros* is often the daughter of the priest in charge, presumably dragged in for the small ritual tasks, as an Anglican clergyman might induce his son to act as a server in the cult (see Dunand III.164). And even if more information was available about the acts open to priestesses, the general preliminary questions must still be raised, in respect of the nature of the religion in question. Where does religious power lie? Jews and Christians wait to hear the Law and the Word, and he who has authority to expound it and teach it has power over their minds: he who has authority to perform the cultic acts (eg. the sacraments) has power over their belonging to the group, exercised through the administration of circumcision or baptism, for example. Is the Isis cult a religion of the word, or a religion of ritual where the priests and priestesses have power over the participation of the believers, and therefore over their ability to experience the knowledge of Isis? Is the language or the ritual the key to religious power? Such questions must be answered first, and possibly invalid analogies with Christianity removed, before the non-existent information about women in the Isiac hierarchy could even be useful. However it is an interesting fact that the role of *oneirocrites* (dream interpreter) was fulfilled by women in both Athens and Delos in the Hellenistic period, the feminine form of the word being *oneirocritis* (see Dunand III.155). The Hellenistic period saw increased interest in all forms of divination, and the demand for knowledge of the future and understanding of the present must have been very great: late in this period the function of dream interpretation became a regular part of the Isiac cult. Almost no-one seriously disputed the idea that a correct interpretation of dreams (or of many other natural phenomena) could yield true knowledge, and philosophers tended to agree on a general view of divination, irrespective of their background. Philo, a Hellenistic Jewish writer, gives much the same discussion of the phenomenon as Cicero: at the end of the second century AD, the Christian writer Clement of Alexandria gives a list of Hebrew prophets to be compared with a list of accredited Greek prophets, but nowhere does he suggest that the Greek prophets uttered falsehood. Such a view was not necessary: Stoicism provides a rationale for divination, which linked phenomena such as dreams to the laws of nature, and their interpretation was consequently a matter of objective scientific procedure. We are therefore left with the impression that there was a great development of interest in all forms of sooth-saying in the Hellenistic period, and we know that treatises were frequently written on the subject. We may therefore surmise that the women playing the role of dream interpreters were in a position of considerable authority in the cult, since their ability to explain these nocturnal visitations would have been much in demand. Dunand (III.155) thinks that their function was not important, but this appears to be an arbitrary assumption, linked with a consistent attempt on her part to play down the importance of women in the cult: the only argument she does advance is based on one case where the function of *oneirocrites* was combined with that of the *aretalogos* (ie. reader of the account of the virtues and acts of the Goddess), and she concludes that both must have been of lesser importance for such a combination to be possible. This is scarcely compelling, and it must be supposed that this is a case where the demands of the believing public would determine the power of the female and male dream interpreters, in a case where we have every reason to suppose that these demands must have been very great. It is interesting to note that for Malaise (136-7) the tendency for women to enter the priesthood is a proof of Egyptian influence on the Italian cult, and for Dunand (III.167) such Egyptian influence is the cause of precisely the opposite, namely 'the surprising fact' that 'Isis is not served by an essentially feminine clergy'. There seems to be some confusion over the Egyptians. To sum up, the situation appears to be that we know of priestesses of Isis in the Imperial period; they seem to be in the minority, but we do not know much of the hierarchical structure of the cult, nor of the powers of the priesthood.

One last point should be made. It is quite clear that the religion of Isis provided for the first time in classical antiquity a deity with which women could identify. Her titles (she was called Isis 'of the myriad names') show her as Sister of Osiris, Daughter of Cronos, Widow, Queen, Mother (of Horus, and nature in general) and the Beautiful: in each of the areas of womanly experience, Isis participates by being a woman in that role. She is also the patron goddess of child-birth, of fertility, sailors, life and magic. Her story shows her as having been a prostitute in Tyre: the legend of her marriage to her brother Osiris shows her as mourning over his death and dismemberment, and seeking to recover the pieces of his body, but she is unable to find the phallus. Isis was remarkably comprehensive, and was identified with all kinds of local goddesses as illustrated by Apuleius in Book XI of the *Metamorphoses;* her capacity to meet the aspirations and needs of women was therefore limitless. The religion of Isis seemed to have little in the way of regulative orthodoxy, which might have placed some control on the definition of the goddess' functions. Two famous accounts of Isis in antiquity may be compared: the *On Isis and Osiris* by Plutarch, which provides a philosophical interpretation of Isis as a cosmic principle, and the *Metamorphoses* (or 'Golden Ass') of Apuleius, in which Apuleius' chosen character Lucius finds his salvation from asshood through initiation into the cult of Isis. These writers, and one notes that they are both male, give greatly contrasting prictures of the religion, the former constituting the intellectual's demythologisation, and the latter the intellectual's description of his subjective experience of the goddess.

However the mere fact that the cult provided a deity with which women could identify in no way points to a release from rigidly prescribed roles for them. On the other hand, the question of eligibility for the priesthood, and the nature of this function, is a crucial matter for understanding whether Isis tended to foster flexibility in defining female responsibilities in society. The difference between these two issues is the difference between the question of whether it was power which was offered to women, or comfort. Did Isis offer only solace to women, or did she also offer them jobs? There must be a strong presumption that the provision of help in bearing burdens does not always remove the burdens, but rather establishes them more firmly in their position. The question for feminism here is a general one involving the assessment of religion. Satisfaction gained in religion may serve to mute social and political demands; it may simply help to make the unbearable bearable. Is it sufficient to assume that the period when deities were feminised was a paradise for women?

BIBLIOGRAPHY

Baer, R.A. *Philo's use of the categories male and female* (Leiden, Brill 1970).

Beneche, E.F.M. *Antimachus of Colophon: Women in Greek Poetry* (Bouma, repr. 1970).

Dunand, F. *Le culte d'Isis dans le bassin oriental de la Méditerranée,* 3 vols. (Brill 1973).

Daube, D. *Gewaltloser Frauenwiderstand im Altertum* (Konstanzer Universitätsreden 1971).

Fantham, E. *Sex, Status and Survival in Hellenistic Athens: a Study of Women in New Comedy;* Phoenix 29 (1975) 44-75.

Heyob, S.K. *The Cult of Isis among women in the Graeco-Roman World* (Brill 1975).

Malaise, M. *Les conditions de pénétration et de diffusion des cultes égyptiens en Italie* (Brill 1972).

Philo. May be consulted in the Loeb Classical Library.

Chapter Two

Androgynous motifs, hermaphrodites, and the sex of the gods

Early Christian literature abounds in references to androgyny (the state of being both male and female) and androgynous deities, though this is not true of the New Testament documents. The motif is conspicuously absent from this body of documents, and is therefore more to be associated with those schools of Christian thought commonly referred to as 'heterodox': however the question of the interpretation of *Galatians* 3.28, where Paul states that in Christ there is neither male nor female, must be dealt with in this context, since it is possible that here the general preoccupation with the androgynous might have surfaced even in the New Testament documents. At first sight, of course, this verse is taken as suggesting asexuality rather than bisexuality, and this issue will be examined later, together with the later Christian interpretation of the verse.

Interest in the androgynous surfaces from time to time in Western culture, and it has been the subject of an essay by Mircea Eliade (*Mephistopheles and the Androgyne, or the Mystery of the Whole,* in *The Two and the One*), who dwells on the idea of the unification of opposites illustrated in the androgyne's combination of female and male sexuality. Medical definitions of androgyny or hermaphroditism (the hermaphrodite is a person with male and female organs, called after the mythical son of Hermes and Aphrodite) are complex, and involve many variations. It is clear that androgyny is part of nature, and is not limited to human religious speculation: hermaphrodites exist, not only among human beings, but also among as diverse phenomena as marihuana plants and goats. Eliade points to the tendency in mystical theology to defy the limits of ordinary thought, and refers to Nicolas of Cusa's belief that God could be best understood through a description involving the 'coincidentia oppositorum'. Heracleitus' fragment 67 is cited: 'God is day and night, winter summer, war peace, satiety hunger — all the opposites, this is the meaning'. In this way the idea of a mysterious, transcendent God is communicated through a mind-jolting combination of opposing concepts, and it is clear that the interest of the notion of the androgynous is that it suggests completeness, and that a lack has been overcome. In this view, being either male or female is like being either left-handed or right-handed, in that it might be better to be both, that is, ambidextrous. Sexual individuation is seen as the imposition of limits, and maleness and femaleness are both states which are indigent. Androgyny symbolises a totality which holds all possibilities within itself. Eliade (100) regards the Romantic interest in the androgyne as a form of decline, since the 19th century Decadents were more interested in its physical representation, the hermaphrodite. The sexual conundrums arising out of interaction with the hermaphrodite were the main focus of interest, and for Eliade such a development is an instance of 'the degradation of the symbol'. There appears to be a suggestion here on Eliade's part that the androgyne motif is only of interest so long as it is confined to the other-worldly and the metaphysical, and that the sheerly physical reaction to the hermaphrodite lacks this transcendent aspect: one should be cautious about this, since human sexual experience has not always been dissociated from the path to the divine in the Western tradition. Plato's *Symposium,* and the later Platonist Plotinus both present human sexual love in the context of higher aspirations, and as providing a model and a starting-point for love of the divine. Thus the western tradition provides us with the possibility of developing a philosophy of sexual relations which avoids treating them as intellectually insignificant.

Even the 19th century writer Péladan, whose work has been described as a 'veritable encyclopaedia of the taste of the Decadents' (Mario Praz, *The Romantic Agony* 359), and who uses the theme of the androgyne constantly (*L'Androgyne* 1891) does not trivialise the concept into a mere form of titillation, but universalises it to claim it as perfection, the overcoming and transcending of polarised sexuality. Not that the specific results of contact with the hermaphrodite are passed over; on the contrary the source of frustration, and the sense that one can neither satisfy nor be satisfied by the hermaphrodite is dwelt on, and this is the key to the frequent suggestion that androgyny is asexual, because it seems to be out of a normal pattern of sexual interaction. For Péladan the exploration of these physical limits led to a broad philosophy of androgyny (see the *Erotologie de Platon* in the *Amphithéâtre des sciences mortes,* and *L'Androgyne*), in which for example, the androgynous is said to be the sex of the artistic temperament because it combines masculine and feminine capacities, and reference is also made to a form of ethical androgyny, which combines the ethical authority of man with the desire of woman.

These ideas are capable of further development, and they have been discussed here because they provide insights into what may have been the roots of the interest in the androgynous motif in late antiquity and in Gnostic Christianity. In many respects the Decadents and the Gnostics are comparable, and in respect of this particular issue, the significance of the androgynous, there are marked similarities, which will be looked at in detail. Bisexual deities had been known in Egyptian mythology; the High God Atum was called the He/She, and generated single-handed a brother and sister, the first male and female. In the Coffin Texts, II.161 ff, Atum is referred to as 'he', and then as having 'given birth' to Shu, his bisexuality thus being underlined. Hapi, the spirit of the Nile, is bisexual.

In the Greek tradition, the idea of an androgynous principle is particularly identified with Plato's *Symposium* and the speech of Aristophanes in that dialogue. However the idea of the androgyne is rooted in Greek culture with the myth of Hermaphrodite, the bisexual progeny of Hermes and Aphrodite. These two were thought to be brother and sister, and both were the children of Ouranos (the sky). Their child, Eros (love/desire), had been entrusted to the nymphs of Mount Ida. He resembled both his mother and father, and was a creature of singular beauty. While travelling in Caria, he was seen by the nymph Salmakis, who fell in love with him. Though he resisted her love, he fell into the waters of her fountain: she thus embraced him and became one with him. In this way he became a true man-woman. (The myth of Narcissus is also a story of unrequited love, but which reaches no successful conclusion, since Narcissus, in love with his own image and therefore incapable of finding satisfaction, pined away and died.) Some of the older classicists look with horror on this Greek interest in the hermaphrodite. 'Monstrosities', says H. J. Rose (A Handbook of Greek Mythology 148), and treats interest in the androgyne as a symptom of decadence in the late Greek world. Similarly Farnell (Cults of the Greek States II.628) speaks of the 'darker side' of the worship of Cybele, and 'that strange idea of the confusion of sex, the blending of the male and female natures in one divine person'. Farnell refers to evidence that a bearded Aphrodite was worshipped in Pamphylia, and to the bearded Aphrodite (or Venus) in Cyprus. Macrobius (Sat. 3.8) describes the latter in detail.

However the late Greek period, or the Hellenistic age, saw a great deal of interest in the hermaphrodite and the whole idea of bisexuality. Hermaphroditic representations in art stood side by side with a tendency to define God as bisexual, and the idea that these two facts should be connected is irresistible. In the Paris Louvre there may be seen a sculpture of a reclining hermaphrodite on a luxurious couch, with hair in an elaborate coiffure, arms folded and head down, asleep, with soft sensual lines, rounded, yet having the frame of a slim figure. A cloak hangs loosely from one arm, revealing the naked body, and the whole creation is unmistakeably sensual. The hermaphrodite is so situated in the Louvre as to cause many people to pass behind it, noticing the feminine lines of the body, but in many cases not bothering to move to the other side, thereby failing to see the penis. Those who do react in various ways, some with affected unconcern, some with nervous titters, and others with overt disgust. There is in fact something which is absolutely arresting about the sculpture and which almost always produces a strong reaction in people who look at it, and there are many, one suspects, for whom the very idea is repugnant. Is the overt sensuality of this hermaphrodite an indication, as Eliade would claim, of the degradation of a symbol? It is certainly true that in this late Greek period, there was considerable philosophical and theological interest in the idea of a god or highest principle manifesting the characteristics of both the sexes. Whether a sexually provocative hermaphrodite is evidence of a debasement of such high-flown philosophical considerations probably depends on presuppositions concerning the nature of sexuality: a properly developed philosophy of desire would include sexual desire, as well as other forms, as material to be analysed. The usual Platonic view incorporates sexual desire as part of a general philosophy of the attraction of beautiful things, whether of a higher or a lower kind, and the hermaphrodite raises interesting issues about the nature of desire. (These same issues were felt to be present by the Romantics, with their interest in the physical androgyne; despite Eliade, they show considerable interest in the intellectual conundrums thrown up by androgynous sexuality.)

The hermaphrodite may attract, yet repel: will satisfy, yet not satisfy; will be satisfied, yet not satisfied. Ordinary sexual desire, whether homosexual or heterosexual, is confronted with offering incomplete satisfaction, or receiving incomplete satisfaction. A man may seek the femininity of the male/female, or may be drawn to its maleness, yet the presence of the other identity will offend, or be present as an element which is irrelevant, yet related to the sexual experience. The hermaphrodite has a magnetism which terminates in impenetrability, and this is what makes it fascinating as an image to be applied to the deity. Feminists speak of the problems arising from characterising God as male, and in the case of this set of late Greek ideas, we have an approach which deals directly with this problem in quite an interesting way. Pliny (*Natural History* VII.3.34) tells us that in Roman times hermaphrodites were regarded as entertainment, but that in earlier times they were called *androgyni,* and were regarded as portents. A portent, or *prodigium,* is usually a sign of something; it is a phenomenon inviting interpretation. Clearly then, whilst the hermaphrodite may have become a spectacle, in the late Greek period it was seriously considered as a key to some truth about reality.

Can we piece together the elements of this late Classical (and early Christian) concern with the bisexual? Art historians agree that the sculptor's interest in the hermaphrodite is specific to the late Greek period, and many are very quick to give this as evidence for a decline in Greek sensibilities. But as is often the case, moral judgments obscure complex events which need to be understood, and it is clear that some neutral way of assessing this new trend must be found. The artistic representations are accompanied by a general intellectual interest in the idea of androgyny, and one of the prime passages to be discussed here is the already mentioned speech of Aristophanes in Plato's *Symposium*. Though it is intended to be comic it reflects quite accurately the Greek understanding of the predicament of sexual love.

Aristophanes claims (189D) that in the first place there were three kinds of human beings, the two sexes, and a third kind, the man-woman. The man-woman is born of the moon, since the moon partakes of both the sun and the earth, which are the substance of the male and female respectively. At a certain point the gods cut these creatures in two with the result that each half searches for the other in anguish. The man-woman is divided off into men and women, who pursue each other; the male is divided into men who pursue each other, and the women into women who pursue each other, and thus homosexuals come into existence. The climax of the speech comes at the end of 192C, where love (*eros*) is said to be the desire and pursuit of the state of wholeness. One is therefore said to be in a state of separatedness, with a sense of incompleteness which drives towards the fulfilment of one's desires. Women desiring women, and men desiring men, are in the minority, but for the whole human race the need is the same, namely that of giving love its fulfilment. Love is said to be a means of returning to one's original nature, that is, to one's completeness as a living being. It is love which helps us return to our own existence.

Of course the *Symposium* does not stop there, and other characters speak on the question of love, notably Agathon and Diotima. Agathon begins on premises entirely different from those of Aristophanes' comic speech, and emphasises the contributing aspect of Love, whereas the previous speaker had presented is as a state of need, or privation. Thus for Agathon, 'Love was originally of surpassing beauty and goodness, and subsequently became the cause of similar qualities in others' (197). Love is thus concerned with enhancing the other, as well as with seeking it. The speech of Diotima brings yet another refinement, since Love is presented as the child of Poverty and Resource (the Greek word *poros* combining the ideas of

Hermaphrodite, Hellenistic (Louvre, Paris).

resources and the possibility of achievement). 'Love is neither without resource nor in a state of plenty at any one time' (203E): it is in a state of intermediate tension. It is not the state of absolute penury, as with Aristophanes' characterisation, since it has the positive aspect of seeking and scheming for all that is good. But Love is also homeless, unshod, and in need (203D). It combines lack and need, with striving and creativity. Plotinus, the third century A.D. disciple of Plato, puts the point in this way:

> Love is a mixed thing; being in need, for which reason it seeks to be fulfilled; but not without a share in plenitude, for which reason it seeks that which is missing from what it already possesses. (III.5 (50).9)

Plotinus also says

> Love is like a goad, without resources in its own nature. Even when it attains its goal, it is once more without resources. (III.5 (50). 7)

This is the characterisation of love that we find in the Greek philosophers, and it does much to explain the preoccupation with the bisexual, or androgynous, in less pure forms of philosophical literature. Love is considered to be the expression of lack; it is a symptom of incompleteness. It would be astonishing to find in Plato and Plotinus any suggestion that the forms or any of the higher principles (hypostases) were bisexual, since such an idea would be far too close to mythical thinking. However in the more popular movements, where a connection between ordinary religion and philosophical thought had developed, it is not surprising to discover speculation on androgynous divinities and principles. (We may note however in this connection that Plotinus does allegorically consider the idea of making Zeus and Aphrodite a composite being, in the course of his interpretation of Plato's Symposium. Plotinus' language is to be taken figuratively, but he suggests that Aphrodite could be understood as the soul of Zeus; III.5 (50). 8).

The Pythagorean tables of opposites contrasted various cosmic realities such as night and day, male and female, and it is therefore natural that some effort should have been made to transcend these polarities. The impulse in religious thought to transcend opposites has therefore frequently been attributed to Pythagorean tendencies, or the desire to react against

Pythagorean influences. The term male/female (*arsenothelus*), as applied to the highest principle, or the One, is seen as just such an effort to overcome the tension of opposites in which the cosmos is caught. We are told by Iamblichus (*Theolog. Arithm.*, de Falco, 3.21) that the Pythagoreans call their monad God, and also male/female. This monad, or unity, is both odd and even, and also both father and mother, and seems to be the source of both matter and form. Festugière (*La Révélation* ..., 43) is inclined to suspect that Stoic influences are present as well as Pythagorean, in the presentation of the ultimate God as male/female, and he cites Augustine's *City of God* (VII.9), where Valerius Soranus, a contemporary of Cicero, is quoted to the effect that Jupiter is both father and mother of the Gods. Well prior to him, Aristotle had outlined the doctrines of the Pythagoreans (*Metaphysics* 986 a 15) in a way which elucidates the tendency to combine male and female. The elements of number are said to be the odd and the even, and the One is said to be composed of them both. In this way the One of course becomes the source of numbers, and then of the whole of reality, but according to Aristotle, the Pythagoreans also assimilated the male with the odd number, and the female with the even. It follows then that the One would transcend this sexual opposition as well, or alternatively, combine both sides within itself. Finally, Festugière also demonstrates that the expression *Zeus arren, Zeus thelus* (Zeus male, Zeus female) was well-known in Greek at the time.

In this material there is a clear focus on the generative capacity of a single bi-sexual god, and the need of both sexes for each other in order to procreate, leads to the suggestion that God or the One, who engenders the universe, is a complete being because he combines in one being capacities which on the human level imply some interdependence. But this emphasis on the generative capacity of God is not the only stimulus towards the presentation of God as androgynous: the Platonic understanding of desire, outlined earlier, also has its part to play.

In Valentinian Gnosticism the goddess Sophia has an enormously revealing role to play. She is one of the principles, or hypostases, of reality, which the Gnostics tend to personalise into deities, giving them names. The tragic portrait of the female Sophia will be discussed in the next chapter, but here it may be noted that her chief affliction is passion. Valentinian Gnosticism, whether or not it is considered to be a branch of Christianity, is impregnated with Greek philosophy, and the Greek understanding of desire as a lack, a need for fulfilment, is the essence of the predicament of Sophia. Her consort is the 'desired one', and this female principle is the very archetype of unfulfilled desire. She desires, but desires in vain and from a kind of audacity, since she is not really able to come close to the real Desired One, that is, the true and perfect Father. (Sophia is described as an aeon, which is born of another principle called the Duodecad: in descent, she is so far removed from the essence of things, that her attempts to explore it are doomed to failure.) Sophia reaches out constantly towards this essence of things, but by her nature is incapable of reaching it. Consequently she is in distress, and her state is bereft. She is reaching for something that she will not attain. Irenaeus records (*Adv. Haer.* I 1,2.1), referring to the system of Ptolemaeus, that because she had undertaken an impossible task, she was in very deep distress, owing to the greatness of the depth and the inscrutability of the Father, and because of her love for him. Sophia then extends herself further until she reaches the point where limits impose themselves, despite her own will and impulsion, and these limits are personified in the Gnostic system by Horos (Limit). Sophia encounters Horos abruptly; repulsed, she falls back into the realisation that the Father is incomprehensible. Ptolemaeus, whose system of thought this is, thus informs us that the object of desire is knowledge.

The tragedy of Sophia, one of the most remarkable myths of womanhood in ancient literature, will be dealt with in greater detail in the next chapter, but it has been referred to here in order to demonstrate the importance of the passion/desire motif. The acute condition of Sophia's distress is her desire, and this constitutes an orientation towards an outside object (in this case, the Father God) which is beyond reach. Her anguish is thus a direct product of her desire, and it is the centrality of the understanding of desire as the state of being bereft which gives us the clue to the emphasis on androgyny, bisexuality and hermaphroditism. These are states of completeness, in which desire is abrogated because the lack which engenders it, is not present. Sophia encounters Horos (Limit) who places around her boundaries which inhibit, but do not satisfy. (The meaning of Horos will be discussed in the next chapter.)

It is such an understanding of desire which lies behind the emphasis on bisexual divinities in the late Hellenistic age. In Gnostic thought one inevitably encounters a bisexual principle at some point, though rarely at the absolute apex of the mythological hierarchy. In Valentinian thought the principle Buthos (primal cause) comes into existence after the Eight-entity, the Ogdoad. Buthos, together with Sige (silence), emerges after the eight entities in this prior being, and is variously represented in Valentinian thought as alone; not only alone but nothing; asexual; and as male/female. In some versions, Irenaeus tell us (*Adv. Haer.* I. II, 5 ff.), Buthos was considered to have formed a couple with Sige (silence), so that a marriage could have occurred whereby the rest of reality could have been produced. In Gnostic thought such comings-together are called 'syzygies', and the marriage relationship tends to be the habitual model in this branch of Hellenistic 'philosophy'. We are told that some wished to deny that Buthos was bisexual, and saw him as linked with two female principles, entitled Thought and Will. These principles are in fact potentialities in Buthos, since he first takes Thought, and then puts into effect his Will. By the conjunction of the two, Intelligence and Truth are born. Thus is exhibited the typical pattern of Gnostic emanationism; realities are born from higher realities, and all these realities seem to be important categories in human experience and existence. Such an understanding of the production of reality could be termed procreational, and many other examples of this procreational understanding of the ontological process can be cited.

The whole tendency to sexualise theological imagery, especially in a system with a multiplicity of gods and principles, should be evident to anyone reading the Gnostic documents but there is nothing particularly surprising about it, given similar tendencies in Egyptian and Greek mythologies. In Hippolytus' account of Valentinian thought, the Father is described as procreating single-handed, and it is from this unique source that spring all the principles constituting the leading essences of reality (Ref. VI. 30.6; Foerster/Wilson 187). Sophia wishes to emulate this single-handed procreation, but is unable to, not so much because she is a woman, but because she is part of the begotten world, that which has 'become'. The Valentinian system here used a Platonic distinction between that which is unbegotten, and that which is begotten; another way of putting the distinction, which may be found in Plato's *Timaeus* is to say that there are some things subject to a permanent process of becoming, and others which are outside becoming. Because the Father, in this case, is outside the process, he procreates single-handed, but for begotten creatures, procreation is the result of a partnership between male and female. Sophia's efforts are therefore abortive.

The use of this philosophical concept to differentiate between different types of procreation reveals to us that which is considered to be the inferior process in the myth outlined above. Procreation à deux, in which two separate entities must complement each other, is part of the interior ontological state. Individuated sexuality therefore forms part of a deficient state of being, and for this reason Gnostic systems give a considerable place to bisexual beings. Whilst the ultimate divinities are considered to transcend sexuality (although they do procreate), among those deities which lie beneath them, but which are considered to have some particular quality of superiority over others, there are often found beings combining both male and female characteristics. In this way the special quality of the ultimate is reproduced in lesser form on a lower level, and this, as is happens, is an example of the main principle governing the Neoplatonic ontology, or theory of reality.

Representations of the original Adam as bisexual are therefore not uncommon in this period, and it has already been noted that Philo believed in the existence of an original Adam of this kind. Some Valentinian Gnostics (Irenaeus, *Adv. Haer*, I.18.2; Foerster/Wilson 214) distinguishes between two primal men, one formed on the eighth day, the other on the sixth. Some of those wishing to draw such a distinction claimed that the former was the man said to be made 'in the image and likeness of God' (*Gen.* 1.27), and this man was 'male/female'. One can only assume that his bisexuality is a kind of copy of the completeness of God himself. Clement of Alexandria also attests this theme in Valentinian thought (*Excerpta ex Theodoto* 21.1; Foerster/Wilson 224), though the system described is slightly different. However Adam possesses initially both the male and female seed, and

Aphrodite, Hellenistic (Topkapi Museum, Istanbul). A certain grace and feminity shows the departure from the remote classical style.

when this is taken from him, Eve is produced. There is here also an allusion to the female becoming male, this being understood as a spiritual improvement. The essence of the idea of bisexuality is unity, and this is emphasised repeatedly, particularly in Valentinian documents where one might suppose the influence of middle-Platonic and Neoplatonic ideas of unity. Epiphanius' account (*Panarion* 31.5.3; Foerster/Wilson 234) describes the Father (or the unbegotten principle) as both male and female. He possessed *within* himself a female principle called Ennoia, who encouraged him to seek repose by uniting with her, and thereby producing man. *The Megale Apophasis,* also a highly philosophical Gnostic document, emphasises two powers which spring from a single source, one of these powers being the mind of the universe, and of the male sex, the other being female, generating all things. Between them stands the Father, a male/female power which exists in unity. This unity is in fact a duality, since it contains both the male and female potencies: it is interesting to note the overt statement of duality here, since sometimes there is confusion over the question of whether bisexuality is in fact intended to convey asexuality. Here the emphasis is clearly on the two-in-one character of the god. Mind is the equivalent of male, and Conception of the female, but it is noted that though these are two powers, they are inseparable from one another. The *Tripartite Tractate* (132; Robinson 95) deals with the question of the annulment of sexual individuation as follows (trans. Attridge and Mueller):

> For when we confessed the kingdom which is in Christ, we escaped from the whole multiplicity of forms and from inequality and change. For the end will receive a unitary existence just as the beginning, where there is no male nor female, nor slave and free, nor circumcision and uncircumcision, neither angel nor man, but Christ is all in all. What is the form of the one who did not exist at first? It will be found that he will exist, and what is the nature of the one who was not a slave? He will take a place with a free man ... The restoration to that which used to be is a unity.

This document, considered to have affinities with Valentinian Gnosticism, makes much use of philosophical concepts, and links them with an understanding of a principle also enunciated by Paul, in *Galatians* 3.28. Social divisions along the lines of freedom versus slavery, and masculinity versus femininity are abolished in the new life. The emphasis on existence as a state independent of other qualities, and opposed to the state in which one is subject to inequality and change, reveals a Platonic distinction between Being and Becoming; the emphasis on unity reveals a Neoplatonic ontology, where Unity is pitted against Multiplicity. One could compare the *Tripartite Tractate* view of the beatific state with Plotinus, *Enn*. 5.5.4.

On this view the importance of bisexuality may be transcended, since it is claimed that there is no 'male or female', and the perfect state envisaged may be that of asexuality. This is far from assured, since statements of transcendence of this kind often include the juxtaposition of opposites, both of them coming together in an exceptional mode of existence, so that a slave would be both a slave and a free man in this new state. The juxtaposition of opposites in the highest level of existence is characteristic of the passage of Plotinus referred to above, where it said that the small is great, that each is all and all is each, that the sun is the stars, and the stars are the sun. In a Gnostic context, the tendency to bring together contradictions in the highest being is very well attested by the system of Monoimus (Hippolytus, *Ref*. 8.12.1; Foerster/Wilson 247), in which the highest Man is alleged to be a single unity, indivisible, peaceful yet hostile, similar and dissimilar. He is also both mother and father, and compared to the letter iota, which being composed of a single stroke is a unity, yet a unity which is composed of many parts.

We have here quite a striking development of the philosophy of unity as reinterpreted from Plato's Parmenides, in which a secondary type of unity was discussed, involving completeness, and where all parts were present. The tendency in the above Gnostic passage is to reinterpret this secondary unity as a unity which derives its oneness from the presence of a complete set of its parts, to be sure, but where some of its parts are contradictions of each other. This probably reflects a Neopythagorean redefinition of the Parmenidean secondary unity, and such an approach is not frequently found among the more scholastic (or 'orthodox') exponents of the Parmenidean unities.

Clearly the Gnostic preoccupation with bisexual principles

must be explained by this preoccupation with unity as a means of reconciling warring opposites. Where the possibility of a higher principle being asexual is brought forward, the suggestion is that the unity envisaged is one which transcends these opposites. Whilst we have two distinct approaches here, it is not clear that they are ultimately very different: in both cases there is an attempt to escape the solitude of an individuated existence. To be something is to fail to be something else, and this failure is felt as a lack, a conscious state of not-being, or of not being that something else. Being male, or female, is an excellent example of the isolation of such sexual individuality, all the more appropriate since the sexes seem to testify to this solitude by moving towards each other in order to have coition. Sexual love is the sign of a felt lack, and the whole Greek understanding of love (eros) lies behind this example. Gnostic theological imagery combines a Greek understanding of eros with a Greek understanding of unity in order to arrive at an endorsement of bisexuality in the deities of the Gnostic world.

What is the significance of this for the estimate of womanhood? Gnostic imagery contains a great deal which presents woman as weak, subject to passions, and unable to act; this will be dealt with in the next chapter, and to this extent it approaches the very harsh verdict on the image of woman in the writings of Philo, for example. But on the other hand, there is much less of this material, and only rarely does one find the process of spiritual regeneration equated with the process of becoming male. Where the feminine is used as a metaphor for some principle in Gnostic writings, it is often the case that the principle involved is of great significance, and cannot be dismissed as inferior or lesser. Often a female principle stands for faculties which would be regarded as male by Philo, an example being the principle of Ennoia in Valentinian Gnosticism, and there are many cases of male beings who are caught in distress and incapacity. It is clear that the sexual imagery of the Gnostics is not nearly as weighted towards the male as that of Philo, though it cannot be said that it has the opposite tendency. The Gnostics are interested in androgyny, rather than the feminine.

Lastly it must be noted that the use of the bisexual in theological imagery provides an admission that deities need not be thought of as male in order to project an image of perfection.

The abundance of bisexual deities in Gnostic thought constitutes a feminisation of the divine, and quite possibly a reaction against the patriarchal and masculine theological imagery of Judaism. The rugged masculinity of the Hebrew Jehovah is mitigated by a host of intermediary bisexual deities, who combine in themselves what were thought of male and female characteristics. There is clearly a trend here in late Greek religious and philosophical thought, and the emergence of the hermaphrodite as a specifically late Greek subject for sculpture is the clearest proof of this.

Bibliography

Eliade, Mircea, *Mephistopheles and the Androgyne*, in *The Two and the One* (Harvill Press 1965).

Plato, *Symposium*, or *Banquet* (this work may be read in the Loeb Classical Library edition).

Macrobius, *Saturnalia* (trans. P. V. Davies, 1969).

Iamblichus, *Theologoumena tes arithmetikes*, ed. V. de Falco (1922) (Greek only).

Festugière, A.J. *La révélation d'Hermès Trismégiste*, IV (Paris 1954).

Irenaeus, *Adversus Haereses*. This work contains an account and refutation of various Gnostic systems. It may be read in English in volume 1 of the *Ante-Nicene Fathers* (Eerdmans 1973), under the title *Irenaeus Against Heresies*.

Hippolytus, *Refutatio*. As for Irenaeus, but see Volume 5 under the title *The Refutation of All Heresies*.

Foerster, W. (trans. R. Mcl. Wilson) *Gnosis,* vols. 1 and 2 (Oxford 1972 and 1974). A collection of Gnostic sources.

Robinson, J.M. (ed.) The Nag Hammadi Library (Harper and Row 1977).

See also:

Whittaker, J. *Neopythagoreanism and the Transcendent Absolute;* Symbolae Osloenses 48 (1973) 77-86.

Rist, J.M. *Eros and Psyche* (Toronto 1964).

Meeks, W.M. *The Image of the Androgyne: some uses of a symbol in earliest Christianity;* History of Religions 13 (1974) 165-208.

Tardieu, M. *Trois mythes gnostiques* (Paris 1974).

Chapter Three

Earliest Christianity and Gnosticism

There are great differences between the documents of early Christianity on the matter of women and their representation. On the one hand we must deal with the New Testament documents, since these are the ones which have been decreed to be the basis of Christianity over centuries of church councils and theological debate. But is is clear that they alone do not provide a complete picture of what Christianity was in the first two centuries. The ordinary historian will wish to direct his attention to the whole spectrum of the Christian movement in the first two centuries, and to documents which emerge both at the same time as those of the New Testament, and a little later. There should be no strict cut-off point either in terms of time of writing, or in terms of content. Thus the expression 'earliest Christianity' is intended to embrace the study of both the Gnostic sources and the Apostolic fathers, though the theologian preoccupied with solving modern problems, or seeking to bolster some position on the role of women in the church and society, would define his sources more strictly. The description of ancient Christianity and the solution of modern theological problems within the church, are two tasks which are methodologically quite distinct.

The New Testament documents

The New Testament lets us see some distance into the social roles occupied by women within the apostolic church: the book of Acts and some of Paul's letters indicate that certain middle to upper-class women acted as patronesses for itinerant Christian missionaries, thereby providing a ready-made field of contact for them in various cities (see E. A. Judge). They must have been quite important in the expansion process of early Christianity, but quite what conclusion may be drawn from this is not absolutely clear. In the first place, their role as social facilitators and hostesses in relation to society at large was probably not matched by any similar prominence in the organization of the *ecclesia* (church). Secondly, some have inferred that apostolic contact with such women shows that Christianity may not have emerged from the lower strata of society, as is widely believed, but was influential from the outset among the middle and upper classes: to the contrary, however, the importance of the patronesses testifies to the irregularity of Christianity as a social movement. The fact that the Christian missionaries went to the wives rather than the husbands shows, given the ancient context, that they represented a movement which had to gain entry into respectable circles through the back door. The argument for the upper-class pedigree of earliest Christianity would have been immeasurably strengthened had the patronesses been patrons, and one must rather see the apostle as grabbing at whatever social landing-grounds became available to them. They would no doubt have preferred to be hosted by the merchants and administrators who were the husbands of these ladies, but they were in no position to be fussy. One can well imagine how the women, held down in the rigid patriarchal system of the Jewish, Greek and Roman world, might have been seeking solace and satisfaction in the new religion: they may have been casting about for leisure activities and surreptitious dabblings to be carried out without the knowledge or approval of their husbands. Indeed Celsus, the second-century opponent of Christianity, expresses explicit concern over the way in which Christianity was bringing the normal channels of authority in the family and society to collapse. The appeal of Christianity to women was part of his proof that it was a religion for the gullible (Origen, *Contra Celsum* III. 44; III.55).

There are signs in the New Testament that women had begun to take a prominent role in the churches, and that some need was felt to bring them back into line. It is probable that the importance of the patronesses in the proselytisation process, that is the presentation of Christianity to the world at large, led to a tendency for them to assume and demand certain responsibilities within the administration of the church. The revolutionary character of early Christianity would have enabled such an eruption in the usual pattern of role distribution between the sexes, and after the initial period when everything was new, when liturgy, Church order and theology were still being created, it is likely that a need was then felt to return to normal in respect of social matters. Thus I *Timothy* 2, 9-12 advises women to dress and behave modestly, to keep silence, not to attempt to teach, and not to attempt to dominate men, because 'Adam was first formed, then Eve', and because Eve was deceived, while Adam was not. It will be seen in the next chapter that the relative culpability of Adam and Eve proved a matter for debate in later Christianity, but Paul is clearly invoking the Eve model in order to place constraints on active women within the church. Similarly Paul discusses the Christian wife in I *Corinthians* 11: 2-10, and presents a hierarchical structure in which Christ is said to be the 'head' of the man, and man the 'head' of woman. The woman is said to be the glory of the man, and it is noted, as in I Timothy, that man was created first, and woman second. In I *Corinthians*: 14.35 it is advocated that if a woman is in doubt over any point, she should ask her husband about it at home, rather than raising the point at the church gathering. This is a disciplinary provision against women in the church context, rather than the family context, but one of its presuppositions should be stressed: it is assumed that the woman will be less intelligent than her husband, who in fact may have been doing all the talking at the church gathering, and may well have been her intellectual inferior.

Paul commands women to be obedient to their husbands (*Colossians* 3.18), but the husbands to love their wives. The command to obey is reiterated for women in *Ephesians* 5.21-24: 'Obey one another in the fear of Christ. Wives should obey their husbands as they do the lord, since man is head of the woman, as Christ is head of the church, and is saviour of the (entire) body. And as the church obeys Christ, so women should obey their husbands in everything'. There is an oddity in the first sentence, which seems to contradict what follows. In the first place people are commanded to obey each other, and then wives are commanded to obey their husbands: the first sentence can only refer to an ethic which is being advocated for males, to the effect that they should be more submissive to each other than hostile.

But no such reciprocal arrangement is advocated for women, who are to obey their husbands. Paul continues by presenting the relation of Christ to the church in the terms of a sexual metaphor, in which Christ is the male, and the church the female. Extending the metaphor (verse 28) Paul claims that men ought to love their wives as their own bodies, and that loving one's wife is like loving one's own self. It is noted that no man ever hates himself, but nourishes and cares for himself: so Christ tends his bride, the church. Verse 31 reverts to the idea that man and woman become 'one flesh' in marriage. Verse 32 exclaims: 'This is a great mystery; but I am dealing with Christ and the church'. In my view the first clause ought to be taken as an expression of wonderment over the wealth of the metaphor being used, over the profound significance of marriage itself, and the second clause as a reminder to both reader and author that Paul is in fact intending to discuss the marriage of Christ and the church, rather than marriage itself.

This passage is one of the rare instances of the use of sexual imagery in the New Testament, and recalls the language of Philo and some Gnostic writings. The idea that man and woman become one in marriage reflects the whole context of interest in sexual individuation discussed in chapter two, and stems from the same trend of thought which leads to theological interest in androgyny and the higher state of asexuality. Valentinian Gnostics took it up as providing an understanding of the marriages which took place within the Pleroma, and they took verse 32 as being in its first part a reference to the mystery of the unification of two bodies in one marriage. In the account given by Irenaeus of the system of Ptolemaeus, Paul is alleged to have spoken about the couplings of the cosmic principles. 'Writing about the sexual union of ordinary live, he says: 'This is a great mystery; but I am speaking of Christ and the church' .' The Gospel of Philip invites us to meditate on the mystery of marriage, and notes that without it the world would not have existed, for the existence of man lies at the origin of the world, and the existence of man depends on marriage. Unclean spirits, male and female, also combine in marriage under various principles. It is clear that the twin notions of sexual desire and sexual union were considered to be profoundly significant for the understanding of the nature of the cosmos (Foerster/Wilson 87;

Robinson 139).

Advice to widows is characteristic of I *Timothy* and *Titus*.
Widows have a specific task assigned them in Titus: the younger
women need to be taught how to love their husbands and
children (*Titus* 2: 4-6). The first letter to Timothy deals
extensively with the duty of widows not to remarry: widows
should devote their days to prayer (5.5). Widowhood thus
becomes a vocation at the service of the church, and it is at
points such as this that one perceived the suspicion of marriage
that underlies some Christian thinking.

As far as Paul is concerned, there is some ambiguity to be
detected in the attitudes expressed. Whilst it has been noted that
he commands silence on the part of women in the churches, it is
also true that he permits women to prophesy. There is a seeming
contradiction here, and it must be noted that Paul regarded
prophecy as one of the important aspects of the Christian cult.
There is a comparison here with the women dream-interpreters of
the religion of Isis, except that there one is not absolutely sure of
the importance of the role of the *oneirocrites*. In the case of the
Christian church, it is clear that Paul regarded the function of
prophecy as very important. The first letter to the Corinthians
(14.4) exhorts one to seek all spiritual gifts, but in particular that
of prophecy. It is to be preferred to the gift of speaking in
tongues. The latter is considered to constitute a rapport between
God and the individual, whereas prophecy is useful for others
and provides generalised communication from God to the
church. There is a ranking of spiritual functions given in I *Cor.*
12.28, and prophecy occurs in second place, after the apostolic
function, and well before such activities as speaking in tongues
and gifts of healing. (The prophetic function, involving
communicating something from God to others, could quite well
be compared to the dream interpretation of the Isiac priestesses,
since the dreams were also held to be direct messages from God
to the human mind).

It is not clear exactly how the permission to prophesy can be
reconciled with the command for women to remain silent in the
churches. It is possible that Paul's thought developed between
these expressions of points of view, or that he had in mind
different aspects of church practice, when making these different
apostolic prescriptions. Most probably the gift of prophecy was

regarded as something exceptional, and the practitioner as being in a special category, so that the sex of the prophet seemed to be a question of very minor significance: in the other case, the prohibition may have been intended to regulate ordinary discussions in church gatherings. The ability to prophesy must have placed women in a different category, not subject to the same limitations as the more ordinary roles.

This is not the only suggestion of a positive role for women in Paul. In I *Cor.* 7.4, in the context of a discussion of celibacy and fornication, it is stated that the 'wife does not rule over her own body, but the husband does; likewise the husband does not rule over his own body, but the wife'. As Robert Banks points out (*Paul and Women's Liberation* 85), this is a particularly distinctive moral position, since a degree of mutuality is insisted upon. The woman has the right to expect that she be properly treated, as well as the man, in the demands they make of each other's bodies. Although the rights of women are safeguarded here, the principle is nevertheless a very heavy one for both parties. Each 'rules over' or 'has power over' the body of the other, and this mutual dominance probably reflects the idea that marriage produces 'one flesh', rather than two parties, each with individual responsibilities towards the other. The crossed lines of authority seem to reflect a notion of marriage different from the idea of a contract between two parties.

Among the more positive elements for women in Paul's teaching, must be included the well-known verses of *Galatians* 3: 27-28: 'For as many of you as have been baptised into Christ have put on Christ. There is neither Jew nor Greek, neither slave nor free man, neither male nor female, for you are all one in Christ Jesus'. The significance of this passage has been hotly debated, since it appears to have some bearing on the question of the ordination of women to the priesthood, and their taking responsibility for other administrative tasks within the church. The later Christian interpretation will be examined in the next chapter, with particular reference to the apparent annulment of the male/female distinction in Christ. Determining what was intended by Paul is a different matter.

In the first place, Paul's statements are addressed to a group of respondents: 'you'. The new state applies to 'as many of you who are baptised into Christ', and so the termination of the social distinctions referred to is not of general application, but applies to those who are 'in Christ' through baptism. Some interpreters move from this point to the argument that Paul's claims about a new state of affairs apply to the church only, but there is a shift in such an argument which needs to be made overt. Paul is not referring to the church in its social manifestations here, nor to any aspect of practical church organisation, nor to any characteristics of the Christian group as a social body. He is referring to changes of state in those who are 'in Christ', and is not making the statements about church order. What social implications he would draw from this statement of metaphysics is another matter, to which we shall return shortly.

It should also be noted that there is not so much a statement of equality in verse 28, as of unity (see Robert Banks 82). If Paul had wanted to bring forward an idea of equality, he would have to have said: 'In Christ there are *both* Jews *and* Greeks, both slaves and free men, both males and females'. Instead he chooses a neither/nor construction which highlights the fact that the new state transcends the old: the old divisions no longer hold. The social divisions are lost in a new unity, which springs from Christ. Now it is clear that a unity can contain many unequal parts, and this is of no significance so long as a totality is achieved: thus it is at least possible that Paul intended to say nothing at all about the equality of the various parts in this new whole. I do not think that this is quite the case, but it is necessary to be aware that the preoccupation with unity was a very dominant perspective in late antiquity. The idea that plurality is the essence of the human predicament, and the pursuit of unity its resolution, is more characteristic of Neoplatonism, but many traces of the antithesis between unity and multiplicity are found in Philo. Talk about the 'warring passions', which may be found in Philo and Paul, often springs from the view that the difficulty encountered by men springs from the fact that they themselves are multiple, rather than one. The sense of division and separation as a plight to be remedied seems to have been very strong, and as we saw in the previous chapter, this theme lay behind the interest in androgyny as a means of overcoming sexual differentiation and unlikeness.

Did Paul mean to make a social comment when he wrote these verses? At first sight it is hard to imagine for what other reason he could have written them, since he chooses the three gravest sources of division in society: racial, class and sexual distinctions. However we must ask what kind of social outlook he might have had, and we must beware of foisting on him the post-enlightenment concerns with equality, social justice and liberty, which are our own instinctive values. Again, he is not so much concerned with equal rights, as classifications which divide people, and make them different from each other, whether equally or unequally. It is possible that Paul had in mind the idea of the original asexual or androgynous Adam, in which case Christ, as the new Adam, would provide the means of returning to this state. After all, on this view, originally mankind was one, and combined both the sexes within himself. But the fact remains that Paul refers to social divisions, and claims that they are annulled in Christ. A consciousness of these class distinctions must have prompted the remark.

This, however, is not to say very much, since the question which one suspects to lie at the heart of modern discussion of the issue is that of whether Paul's remarks entail social consequences, and the desire that they should, leads to the conclusion that they were intended to imply consequences for the organisation of the church, rather than constituting a mere description of the state of being 'in Christ'. One of the Hermetic treatises (IV. 24.8) observes that souls are neither male nor female, which illustrates to us a way of taking Paul's statement in a different way. The Hermetic text simply makes the point that whilst bodies may be distinguishable along sexual lines, souls are not. Paul may simply be saying that there is a higher state of being in Christ, to which these social distinctions are inapplicable, this presumably being the case here and now, and not being intended to apply to some future post-resurrection state. Would such a view entail changes in social behaviour? Probably not.

Stoicism endorsed the idea of equality in a number of contexts, and in the case where the slave is said to be equal to the master, we find that the equality is found on the moral level. In fact the slave may be superior to his master, if he happens to have a higher moral character, evidenced by his lack of greed or lust (See Seneca, *Epistulae Morales* 47.17). The moral equality envisaged here is equivalent to the equality of the 'higher state' found in the Hermetic text, and in what I argue to be the point intended by Paul. Whilst Stoicism was not without its social effects, the Stoic's equality between slaves and their masters does not cause him to endeavour to reproduce this equality on all social levels, by freeing the slave. On the contrary the statement is more conducive to social inertia, since it is claimed that in all important respects, the two parties are already equal. Stoicism had high ethical values, but they were establishment, rather than revolutionary, values. Similarly in Paul's case, the statement of *Galatians* 3.28 cannot have been intended to have any social effects, since in the case of slaves at least, the existing social order is to be preserved. In I *Timothy* 6.1 slaves are commanded to honour their masters, and particular attention (v.2) is paid to the case of a slave who has a Christian master, and who might be tempted to treat him more familiarly. 'And those who have believing masters should not despise them, because they are brothers, but rather serve them because they are faithful and beloved'. There is a specific countermand here to a social reaction towards equality which may have been taking place: on this issue, as well as on the role of women, I *Timothy* is sometimes thought to reflect a later, more considered conservatism on social matters. This is not necessarily so since this conservatism on social roles is not at all inconsistent with statements like that of *Galatians* 3.28: Paul was simply spelling out his view in more detail in the later writing. I would conclude that the description of the spiritual state of being in Christ of *Galatians* 3.28 is not intended by Paul to lead to social changes, but rather to counteract them, since it is being alleged that the social divisions have already, to all intents and purposes, and in all respects which are of any importance, been superseded. To wish to reproduce a spiritual state on the level of the social body would have seemed to Paul to be self-defeating, and fleshly minded. (It will be noted that the Gnostics did try to do this.) It remains to be said that, despite the fact that Paul did not advocate social change because of the low importance he attached to that phenomenon, he was at least aware of harmful social divisions: he simply considers Christians to have reached a state where these divisions no longer do harm, and fade into insignificance.

The *Tripartite Tractate,* a Gnostic text from the Nag Hammadi collection, has an interpretation of the Pauline principle. And this has already been cited in connection with the theme of androgyny (see p. 47). This interpretation claims that confessing Christ has already led to escape from all the contingencies of human existence, such as change, multiplicity, and inequality (Robinson 95). There is an emphasis on the unity which will be achieved in the end, though this should not be taken as an allusion to an eschatological end-point in time. The *Gospel of Philip* also refers to the unification of male and female. Reflecting the idea of the androgynous Adam, the text runs as follows (trans. W. W. Isenberg: Robinson 142):

> If the woman had not separated from the man, she would not die with the man. His separation became the beginning of death. Because of this Christ came to repair the separation which was from the beginning and again unite the two, and to give life to those who died as a result of the separation and unite them. But the woman is united to her husband in the bridal chamber. Indeed those who have united in the bridal chamber will no longer be separated. Thus Eve separated from Adam because she was never united with him in the bridal chamber.

Once again the concern is not with equality, or social roles, but unity, and the desire to recapture an original androgyny. The drive towards this is acted out in marriage. Both these Gnostic texts emphasise the theme of unity.

Colossians 3.11 reiterates the Galatians principle in different terms, and does not refer to the male/female division. Other social divisions are cited (Greek/Jew, circumcised/uncircumcised, barbarian/Scythian, bond/free). All these distinctions disappear when one 'puts on the new man'. Paul is referring to a state of transcendent spiritual unity, in which the things of the earth have no part to play. Verse 5 speaks of the mortification of earthly members, and it is thus that a contrast between the earthly and the spiritual is established. The social divisions are transcended on the level of the spirit, not overcome or mitigated on the level of the social organism, that is, the realm of the earthly.

Gnosticism

Some Gnostic reflections on Paul's thought have been noted, and it is now time to turn in greater detail to that part of the Gnostic image of womanhood not dealt with in chapter 2. There are several caveats: firstly the date of the Nag Hammadi documents, and the Greek documents of which they are translations, is very problematic. Whether the Gnostic gospels were written after, contemporaneously with, or before the New Testament gospels, must remain an obscure issue. Secondly some Gnostic documents are scarcely Christian at all in any recognizable sense, but this is not a matter of great importance except from the point of view of the historical classification of views.

There is much in Gnostic imagery which echoes Philo's portrait of the female, and a great deal to confirm his image of woman as sensuality, desire and flesh, and therefore as spiritually diminished and enfeebled. In the book Baruch, written by a certain Justin, the female power of the All is said to be without foreknowledge, irascible, of dual mind and body, down to the groin a young woman, but with the body of a serpent below that. This incomplete and sinister creature was called 'Eden' and 'Israel', and that Israel should have been portrayed under such hostile feminine imagery gives an indication of anti-Jewish sentiment in this Gnostic writer (Hippolytus, *Ref*. V. 26.1). Simon Magus, an early Gnostic whose links with Christianity are tenuous if they exist at all, was accompanied by a former prostitute from Tyre, called Helena. Simon claimed that she was his first thought, that she was the mother of various cosmic powers such as angels. She was afterwards held back by her offspring, who did not recognize their father: subjected to every kind of abuse, she passed into a variety of female bodies, wandering into various existences. In Irenaeus' account, Simon identified her with Helen of Troy, the subject of Stesichorus' defamatory poem, on account of which he was blinded. Eventually, after constant trials, she became a prostitute. In this story we have an early example of what will later be described as the tragic epic of womanhood, characteristic of Gnosticism, in which a female deity emerges as creative, good, but subject to loss, pain, humiliation and limits (Irenaeus, *Adv. Haer*. I.23.2).

An interpretation of Eve is given in Sethian (or perhaps Ophite) Gnosticism (see Irenaeus, I.30.7). One of the highest gods,

Ialdabaoth, whose name is unexplained, sought together with the six existing powers to create man. When this had been accomplished, Ialdabaoth breathed into him Intelligence and Thought, but as a result of an intrigue by the female Sophia, this sapped him and emptied him of power. The man, thus endowed with these faculties, forsook his parents and turned to the First Man, who stood above Ialdabaoth in priority and importance. Ialdabaoth desired to take his revenge against them, and 'to find means of making man empty through a woman', and brought Eve into existence. Another female principle conspired against Eve, and tempted her into causing Adam to eat of the forbidden tree (cf.Genesis 3:1-7). When they ate, they acquired knowledge of the highest principles, and abandoned their parents. Thus Ialdabaoth was foiled. This tale has several fascinating aspects: firstly, it is clear that the 'Fall' is presented as a gain, since Adam and Eve are enlightened by their actions. Secondly, this takes place contrary to the design of Ialdabaoth, who had intended Eve's approach to Adam to be destructive of him, to 'empty' him, whereas she was in fact the agent of his enlightenment. Thirdly, the women in this myth are portrayed as plotting against their male counterparts, endeavouring in each case to 'empty them of their power'. This idea of the draining of male powers by the female occurs three times in the space of a very short narrative; Sophia is said to have emptied Ialdabaoth of his trace of light, so that he could not use this power against those above. This network of plots and intrigues has the paradoxical result that Eve, though it had been intended that she should 'empty' Adam, in fact leads him to knowledge, the ultimate gift of gnosis.

There are traces also of the Philonic idea that spiritual regeneration can be represented as the process of becoming male. The *Gospel of Thomas* 114 (Robinson 130) has Simon Peter saying that women are not worthy of the gift of life, and a rejoinder from Jesus that Mary can be led into becoming male, so that she can participate in life like men. 'For every woman who will make herself male will enter the Kingdom of Heaven' (trans. Lambdin). The tractate Zostrianos, which describes the ascent of Zostrianos through the various cosmic levels (aeons), his baptism, and his instruction in the names of those who inhabit the heavenly world, makes spiritual release equivalent to escape from the 'bondage of femininity'. One is exhorted to choose 'the

Diana of Ephesus (Selcuk Museum, Turkey).

salvation of masculinity', and remaining female is made equivalent to entrusting oneself to a lower order: 'Do not baptize yourselves with death' (131; Robinson 393; trans. Siever).

The *Tripartite Tractate* (93, Robinson 77) speaks of an aeon in which the Logos established himself: he is the face of one who revealed himself in 'sincerity and attentiveness'. He was in opposition to lower things; there are said to be copies of the faces 'which are forms of maleness, since they are not from the illness which is femaleness, but are from this one who already has left behind the sickness, and who has the name the Church' ...' (trans. Attridge/Mueller). The *Second Treatise of the Great Seth* 65 (Robinson 336) has Christ urging one not to become female, lest you give birth to evil and its brothers: jealousy and division, anger and wrath, fear and a divided heart, and empty, non-existent desire.' This is a most revealing passage, since it stresses the equivalence between femininity and unfulfilled desire, a key aspect of the Gnostic understanding of woman, which will become clearer in the discussion of the tragic figure of Sophia. Together with this one notes that femininity is subject to extremes of emotion, and divisions within the impulses of the heart. The *Zostrianos Tractate* (VIII.1.1; Robinson 369) confirms the equation of femininity with passion: the pilgrimage of Zostrianos takes him away from the darkness of the body, the chaos of soul and the 'femininity of desire'.

The *Tripartite Tractate* (78; Robinson 69) speaks of an aeon who, when he had come forth, became 'weak like a female nature which has abandoned its virility', and the secondary status of woman is strikingly reflected in a passage from the *Gospel of Philip* (78; Robinson 147). It is claimed that the children borne by a woman resemble the man who loves her; it is not her own love for a man which is said to cause resemblances among the children, but the spotlight of his love upon her causes the determination of their type. If her husband loves her, then her children resemble the husband; if an adulterer loves her, then they will resemble him. 'Frequently, if a woman sleeps with her husband out of necessity, while her heart is with the adulterer with whom she usually has intercourse, the child she will bear is born resembling the adulterer' (trans. Isenberg). This fact of life is then given a spiritual interpretation, but in the image the weakness of the woman must be noted. It is thought that she and her reproductive powers are at the beck and call of male attentions; her own contribution to the dynamics of child-bearing is so attenuated, that the male gaze is enough to obliterate it. Nietzsche is a clear heir to this understanding of the weakness of woman, contributed to the West by the conjunction of Judaism, Gnosticism and Greek thought, and he expresses with startling clarity the understanding of woman outlined above.

> The happiness of man is: I will. The woman's happiness is: He will.
> 'Behold, now the world has become perfect!' — thus thinks each woman when she obeys with all her love.
> And woman has to obey and find a depth for her surface. Woman's nature is surface, a changeable stormy film over shallow waters.
> But a man's nature is deep, its torrent roars in subterranean caves: woman senses its power but does not comprehend it.
> (*Thus Spoke Zarathustra* I, Of Old and Young Women)

The portrait of woman in Gnosticism is not entirely negative, and this statement may be surprising in view of Elaine Pagels' claims about the emancipation of women in Gnostic circles, which she sees as a typical feature. She is inclined to see anti-feminine aspects as exceptional: 'Yet exceptions to those patterns do occur. Gnostics were not unanimous in affirming women — nor were the orthodox unanimous in denigrating them. Certain Gnostic texts undeniably speak of the feminine in terms of contempt.' (*The Gnostic Gospels* 66). The position should be put quite differently, however: if we reserve for separate consideration the social issue of the institutional role of women in the Gnostic churches, we may begin with the imagery of the feminine in the Gnostic mythical systems. Here it is the case that the feminine is usually spoken of as weak, underdeveloped and dangerous. When deities are presented as male/female, then the feminine appears in a more favourable light by virtue of its association with maleness: in such cases the two principles reinforce each other, so as to manifest totality and completeness. Yet, unlike the religion of Isis, there is no supreme goddess standing at the apex of the mythical system. Gnosticism is more concerned with androgyny, and is indeed an exploration of masculofemininity in theological imagery. The feminine is not made to stand alone, as it does in the Egyptian religion: Diodorus tells us (I.27) that because of the primacy of Isis in her own mythical family, women in Egypt came to dominate in private social relations. An Oxyrhynchus papyrus (11.1380, 214-16) gives a great deal of information about the identification of Isis with local divinities, and is in the form of a prayer: it contains the words 'Thou didst make the power of women equal to that of men'.

The harvest of positive portraits of the feminine, taken in isolation, is in fact quite meagre. Valentinian Gnosticism allows woman to be the metaphor for thought, and man for will. This alters the typical Philonic equation of woman with flesh, and man with mind. In this case, where we are dealing with the system of Ptolemaeus, the female-represented principle becomes a faculty of Thought, since she is continually yearning after her offspring. Not being able to produce them of herself, she avails herself of the male Will, and so they are born (Irenaeus, *Adv. Haer.* I.12.1.: Foerster/Wilson I, 196). Here the female principle is in need of complementation, but she is not given a low rating on the epistemological scale.

Similarly to the *Ennoia* (thought) of the above passage, the *Apocryphon of John* (22; Robinson 111) has a female *Epinoia* (conception, or intelligence), who hides herself in Adam. She was brought out of Adam, in the manner of the Genesis story, but here the author of the Apocryphon differs explicitly from the Genesis account: a part of the power of the man was passed into the woman, not merely the 'rib-bone'. The new woman, Epinoia, actually enlightens Adam by lifting the veil which lay over his eyes. Thus a female figure is portrayed positively, and a similar appreciation can be deduced from *Asclepius* VI.65, a document which forms part of the Hermetic literature, but which is also part of the Nag Hammadi collection (see Robinson 300). In this passage there is a reflection on the metaphorical significance of sexual intercourse. 'When the semen reaches the climax, it leaps forth. In that moment the female receives the strength of the male; the male for his part receives the strength of the female, while the semen does this'. The interest of this passage lies in the willingness of the author to accord some strength and power to female sexuality: the fertilisation is mutual, and this contrasts with the physiological weakness of the woman as pictured elsewhere.

Other passages on the value of the feminine are cited by Pagels, but the feminine alone is never given primacy. She wishes further to establish a correlation between theology and 'social practice' (60), and the evidence adduced is relatively convincing (though it is admitted that not all movements in which women played an emancipated role had a masculofeminist theodicy). How far the correlation can be proved is difficult to say, since information about the theology of the Gnostics is not matched by equal amounts of social information, whether from Patristic sources, or from the Nag Hammadi documents. It is true however that our sources do seem to speak in general terms of the freedom of women within the Gnostic churches, and so we must suppose it to be a fairly general phenomenon, spreading across the various sects.

The nature of the correlation is more problematic: is a causal relationship being expressed? Is it being suggested that a feminised theology *produces* better conditions for women? Or does the social situation produce the theology? One suspects that a covert appeal for a major revision of Christian theological discourse lies behind the observed correlation, and if so certain remarks may be made. It is more likely that the freedom of women within the Gnostic churches owes its origins to the influence of the Egyptian culture. As noted above our ancient sources attribute feminine emancipation in Egypt to the religion of Isis, but we need not accept these quasi-idealist historical explanations. The fact, however, that women acted with greater freedom and with more rights in Egypt than elsewhere, we may accept. It is probably the encounter with the culture of Northern Africa that produced the variation in the Christian view of the role of women: among the Gnostics they enjoyed similar institutional rights to the women of Isis, taking on the functions of prophetesses, priestesses, healers and evangelists.

Thus the emancipation of women was a longstanding Egyptian phenomenon simply transmitted into Christianity through the Gnostic sects. The social expression of the movement in respect of the role of women varied between Jerusalem and Egypt in much the same way as it might today as between the United States and Greece, for example. The theology of the Gnostics is simply not a sufficient explanation for these behavioural differences, and in any case its frequent denigration of the feminine (underestimated by Pagels in the opinion of the present author) scarcely warrants such a hypothesis. The religion of Isis alone cannot be responsible for the freedom of action allowed women by Egyptian society: the cult of Isis is a Hellenistic phenomenon, and she is simply inserted into the old Egyptian myths from the Pharaonic period. The rise of Isis, and her position of dominance within the families of gods pictured in the Egyptian myths cannot be a cause of female emancipation, but it is certainly an accompanying factor. The strength and energy of the Egyptian queens in the Ptolemaic period may have been a causal factor, in that examples from above in the era of the new Greek modernity could well have played a part in setting standards for the behaviour of women. Cleopatra VII is the best known of these Lagid queens, but Arsinoe II (who died in 270 B.C.) must surely be her rival in claiming our attention. That she was the equal of her husband must have been clear from the thousands of coins used daily in Egypt, since her portrait together with that of her husband appeared on them. She herself inspected Egyptian military defence capability, and the decree of Chremonides (Dittenberger, *Sylloge* I. 434, line 16) tells us that 'King Ptolemy manifestly followed the policy of his ancestors and his sister in his zeal on behalf of the common freedom of the Greeks'. Her leadership is confirmed by a fragment of the historian Memnon, who tells us that she was used to getting her own way (Jacoby, *Fragmente* ... III.434, p.342, 17). These Hellenistic Queens may have done much to influence the expectations of ordinary women, and for the explanation of this we may ultimately have to look to Macedonia, where in the classical period women enjoyed a different status from their counterparts in southern Greece.

In conclusion then, it may be said that there is a disjunction rather than a correlation between the theology of the feminine and the institutional functions of woman in Gnosticism. Though the feminine is incorporated into the Gnostic characterisation of the gods (as it had been in the myths of the Greeks) it does not receive any endorsement, or particular appreciation: on the other hand, it is clear enough that women occupied positions of leadership in the movement in general. This should be attributed to the impact of cultural differences encountered in the area of North Africa and Syria: non-Jewish Christianity had a different social expression.

The tragic epic of womanhood

The Gnostic corpus of literature abounds in metaphors of womanhood, but none is more important than the description of Sophia and her voyage through unfulfilment. There are echoes of this theme in writings other than those which concern the Valentinians, where the myth of Sophia receives its prominence, and these will be dealt with first.

The soul is sometimes treated as a feminine being. The *Authoritative Teaching* 27-28 (Robinson 280) describes the soul as 'she': She is ill, dwelling in a house of poverty, while surrounding matter tries to deprive her of her sight. She seeks to maintain the faculty of sight, to avoid blindness, through use of the Word. She intends her light to overwhelm the hostile forces which are endeavouring to overwhelm her: she tries to enclose her enemies 'in her presence', and bring them down in sleeplessness. The *Authoritative Teaching* returns to the soul in 31, speaking again of her adversaries. They endeavour to exploit her ignorance, deceive her, until she comes together with matter and bears fruit in it, pursuing many desires to which she is drawn in ignorance. The good soul will rise above these things, and in return for the shame and contumely she suffers in this world, she will receive great spiritual gifts. Her body will become impervious to the manipulations of those who deal in bodies, who seek to strike at the soul through the body, and she now has an invisible spiritual body.

The same tendency to describe the pilgrimage of the soul in terms of a metaphor drawn from the drama of existence as a woman, will be found in the *Exegesis on the Soul,* and developed in greater detail (Robinson 180). The soul is said to be female in nature and name, and to have been originally androgynous. She falls into a body, into the hands of robbers who abuse her and seduce her. She prostitutes herself on all sides, and finds only adulterers and dominating masters wherever she turns. Shame comes upon her, and she is no longer capable of acting: she prefers to live in deceit, because shame prevents her from acting. Those who have power over her eventually abandon her, and she becomes desolate. She has nothing left except the offspring of the adulterers, and these are blind, sickly and feeble-minded. There is an identification with Helen of Troy, similar to that referred to earlier, and we might conclude that this Greek myth is a dominant force in shaping the Gnostic myth of the female. In 137 the *Odyssey* (IV.261) is quoted, showing Helen wishing that she could return to her own house, and claiming that Aphrodite had drawn from her own village and husband.

The myth of Helen (a prototype Sophia), it will be recalled, recorded the epic of the life of one of the most beautiful women of her time. She had been abducted by Theseus and Pirithous, and recaptured by her brothers, Castor and Pollux. Ulysses became one of her suitors, but she married Menelaus. She was seduced by Paris and went to Troy, and when Paris was killed in the Trojan war, she returned to Sparta. She lived a miserable old age, and was eventually murdered: her enemies tied her to a tree and strangled her, and the story is celebrated in the *Iliad* 2, and *Odyssey* 4 and 15. The themes of abduction, rescue, seduction and her dreadful death mark the tale of her life, and these are excellent images for the Gnostic myth of the soul. The *Exegesis on the Soul* 128 has the soul admitting to her Father that she has fled her house and desires to return. After her years of abuse and prostitution, she calls for restoration.

> As long as the soul keeps running about everywhere copulating with whomever she meets and defiling herself, she exists suffering her just deserts. But when she perceives the straits she is in and weeps before the Father and repents, then the Father will have mercy on her and he will make her womb turn from the external domain...
>
> (trans. W.C. Robinson; Robinson 183).

The myth of Sophia uses the same image of womanhood, but it is transposed to the level of a goddess, who constitutes one of the higher cosmic principles. In the system of Ptolemaeus, recorded by Irenaeus (*Adv. Haer.* I.4.1; Foerster/Wilson 133), Sophia is removed from the privileged existence of the Pleroma. With her passion (*pathos*) she went into a state of extreme excitation in her new surroundings of empty shadows. She lacked shape and form: she was like an abortion (*ektroma*); she could grasp nothing. She was given form by a merciful Christ, but he gave her no knowledge. Christ left his imprint on her, but departed, and in the absence of the Logos (that is Christ, the principle of knowledge and intelligence), she strains after that which she knows she does not possess. Her unsatisfied passion is contained by limit personified, *Horos*. She was now in a state of constraint, being nothing but unresolved passion (*pathos*). She suffered fear lest life should abandon her, as the Logos had done; she suffered perplexity, since she knew nothing, Eventually, she turned towards him who gave her life.

The account of Hippolytus is similar, with slight variations (*Ref*. VI 30.6; Foerster/Wilson 187). Sophia saw that the Father, presumably bisexual, was creating offspring single-handed. She desired to imitate him, but did not know that she was unable to do so. Her efforts only produced a formless and incomplete substance, and she wept greatly over the abortion (*ektroma*) which she had produced in her ignorance. The Father had pity on her, and endeavoured to console Sophia, and to release her from her sorrow. Christ and the Holy Spirit came to her assistance. Sophia was later separated from Christ, and fell into terror when she realised that he who had given her form, and who had given form to her creations, had left her side. She sought him in great suffering and pleading. Christ had compassion on her, and sent a marriage-partner to relieve her of her passions (*pathe*). Her condition was now that she was subject to the four primary passions: fear, sorrow, distress and entreaty. Her saviour released her from these passions, and he made her emotions into various essences.

This is one of the most remarkable myths of the female psyche in ancient literature, and may well represent a later reworking of the myth of Helen, with all the existential consciousness which we expect to find in Gnosticism. In it we find woman blind-folded, ignorant, incomplete, driven hither and thither by different passions; her attempts to create are abortive, and she is in a perpetual state of unresolved, restless passion. Horos provides a measure of relief from this aimless passion, and her saviour will be he who knows how to release her from her passion, endow her with mind, and give form to her efforts of creation. It is Christ who becomes her lover and supporter, and with him she will be free from the terror and sorrow which beset her.

Valentinus, if he is the originator of the myth of Sophia, shows great imaginative power, and great empathy for the condition of woman. The myth should be read as a set of images which write into the origins of the cosmos and its inhabitants the experience itself of living as a woman. It could be taken as a male dismissal of womanhood, but this would be to rob Valentinus of his insights: he perceives the agony of woman, constricted by and dependent on male rule, as she was in ancient society. He perceives the state to which she has been reduced, and the nightmarish quality of the description of Sophia's tragedy seems to bespeak a sympathetic insight into the condition of the woman of his own time, which he probably understood more clearly than we do. Womanhood was the state of being subject to the four primary passions: fear, sorrow, entreaty and distress.

Bibliography

References in this chapter

Judge, E.A. *The Early Christians as a scholastic community:* Journal of Religious History I (1960) 4-15; (1961) 125-137.

Celsus. To be found in Origen's work, the Contra Celsum. See *Origen. Contra Celsum,* by H. K. Chadwick (Cambridge 1965).

Banks, Robert, *Paul on Women;* Interchange 18 (1976) 81-105.

Hermetic corpus. See *Hermès Trismégiste* I-IV, ed. Nock and Festugière (Paris 1972).

Seneca, The *Epistulae morales* may be consulted in the Loeb Classical Library edition.

Robinson, J.M. (ed.). See previous chapter.

Pagels, Elaine, *The Gnostic Gospels* (Random House, New York 1979).

Dittenberger, W. *Sylloge Inscriptionum Graecarum* (Olms 1960).

Foerster, W. (trans. R. Mcl. Wilson) See previous chapter.

Hippolytus. See previous chapter.

Irenaeus. See previous chapter.

Other works

Allworthy, T.B. *Women in the Apostolic Church* (Cambridge, W. Heffer & Sons 1971).

Barth, Markus, *The Broken Wall: A study of the Epistle to Ephesians* (Chicago, the Judson Press 1959).

Bedale, Stephan, *The Meaning of kephale in the Pauline Epistles; Journal of Theological Studies* N.S.5 (1965) 211-5.

Caird, G.B. *Paul and Women's Liberty;* Bulletin of the John Rylands Library 54 (1972) 268-82.

Cartlidge, D.R. *I Corinthians 7 as a Foundation for a Christian sex ethic;* The Journal of Religion 55 (1975) 220-234.

Donaldson, James, *Woman: Her Position and Influence in Ancient Greece and Rome and among the Early Christians* (London; Longmans, Green & Co., 1907).

Ford, J.M. *Paul the Philogamist: I Cor. 7 in Early Patristic Exegesis:* New Testament Studies II (1965) 326-48.

Sampley, J. Paul, *And The Two Shall Become One Flesh* (Cambridge University Press 1971).

Jacoby, F. *Die Fragmente der griechischen Historiker* (Brill 1964).

Stendahl, Krister, *The Bible and the Role of Women,* trans. E. T. Sander (Philadelphia, Fortress Press 1966, 1971, 1974).

Tavard, G.H. *Women in Christian Tradition* (Notre Dame/ London 1973).

Thiering, Barbara, *Created Second? Aspects of Women's Liberation in Australia* (Adelaide, Griffin Press 1973).

Chapter Four

Later Christianity

As indicated in the preceding chapter, the understanding of the Pauline principle that there is neither male nor female within the unity in Christ, is of cardinal importance for the assessment of the Christian position on women. There are two questions here: the first has been dealt with, and concerns what Paul himself intended to say; and the second is a matter of how Paul's dictum was understood by subsequent writers. The first two volumes of *Biblia Patristica* list fifteen citations of the verse over the first three centuries of Christian writings, and these show a tendency not to apply the statement socially. The *Gospel of Thomas* attributes to Jesus a saying which is obviously based on an understanding of the Pauline principle. On being asked by the disciples when they will enter the kingdom of heaven, Jesus replies:

> When you make the two one, and when you make the inside like the outside, and the above like the below, and when you make the male and female one and the same, so that the male not be male nor the female female...then you will enter the kingdom of heaven.
>
> (22, trans. Lambdin/Robinson 121)

The Gnostic understanding of Paul's idea is thus devoted to the notion of the obliteration of *difference,* since a few cases of contradictory or merely different notions are taken, and the possibility of the annulment of this difference is held out to those who will enter the kingdom of heaven. A similar interpretation is found in the letter to the Corinthians, falsely attributed to

Clement of Rome (II.12.2). Again it is a matter of waiting for the kingdom of God, but this is not put off until some far distant end-time, since it may occur at any moment, from 'hour to hour'. When asked when his kingdom would come, the Lord is alleged to have said:

> When the two shall be one, and the outside as the inside, and the male with the female neither male nor female.

Some interpretative comment is offered on the significance of this saying, and it casts light on what was said in the *Gospel of Thomas*. It is stated that two become one when two persons speak the truth to each other, and thus there is one soul in two bodies 'without dissimulation'. The 'outside' means the body, and the 'inside' the soul, and the two are to exist in harmony, with the soul manifesting itself in good works. The reference to the annulment of male/female sexuality means that 'when a brother sees a sister he should in no way think of her as female, nor she of him as a male'.

A close comparison may be made with a discussion of *Galatians* 3.28 preserved in Clement of Alexandria (*Stromateis* III.13.93.2.). In replying to the views of Cassian, Clement refers to the physical differentiation between male and female. Jesus is alleged to have replied to Salome that she would know the answers to her inquiries when 'the two become one, and the male with the female neither male nor female'. Clement notes that this saying is not found in the four Gospels, but in the Gospel according to the Egyptians, though he in no way rejects its authority, complaining simply that Cassian has failed to understand the saying allegorically (with the female representing desire). This is developed into the idea that we must rid ourselves of desire and appetite in order to find unity in the discipleship of the Word. Paul's verse is then quoted in support. Being neither male nor female is said to mean that we abandon the shape (*schema,* i.e. physical shape, a term also used to describe geometrical shapes) of maleness and femaleness, and that we become one in unity of soul, 'being neither'. The last two words are difficult to interpret: it is unity which is said to be 'neither', but the feminine noun unity (*henosis*) is made to agree with a neuter adjective (*outheteron*). It is probable that we should understand the new state of non-otherness to be that of being neuter.

Clement cites the verse on three other occasions, usually emphasising the unity found after the abolition of the distinctions mentioned by Paul: the first is listed by the authors of the *Biblia Patristica*, but really only constitutes a passing allusion to the idea that we are all one in Christ (*Paedagogus* III.12.101.2). The emphasis on unity is similarly reiterated in the *Protrepticus* (XI.112.3). The starting point is that Christ is not divided, and the statement that there is 'neither barbarian, nor Jew, nor Greek nor male nor female, but a new man', which is itself an amalgamation of verses (see *Gal.* 3.28 and 6.15), is presented as a proof that there is only one command which is universal, and that is reverence towards God. By extrapolation, the formal and recognizable divisions between people are illusory, provided that the unifying attitude of piety is preserved. Similarly in *Stromateis* V.5.30.4 the stress is on the annulment of divisions, but this is one passage in which the tendency to spiritualise the undivided state is not quite so clear.

In fact there is specific reference to justice and equality in the discussion preceding the quotation of Paul's verse. Quoting some verses which deal with justice between men and in cities, Clement proceeds to give the ethic of the Christians. When the disciples were striving for pre-eminence, they were commanded to 'become as little children' (*Matt.*18.3), by which is meant that they should live in equality and simplicity. The principle that in Christ there is neither bond nor free, nor Greek nor Jew is cited, with the conclusion that there is no envy or jealousy in the Christian community. There is a clear social application envisaged for Paul's principle here, but it is essential to note that the element of sexual equality is omitted. The failure to insist on equality between males and females, whilst insisting on harmony and mutual understanding between other divided classes, is very revealing. Clearly this was a very different issue, and it is difficult to imagine Clement managing to extend the principle of social justice to relations between men and women, given the kind of view of womanhood he establishes in the *Paedagogus,* or *Instructor.* Yet another passage does delve more explicitly into the question of relations between the sexes, and this most revealing reflection on *Galatians* 3.28 does not find its way into the *Biblia Patristica* list, possibly because the language does not clearly enough reflect that of any one particular verse. *Stromateis* IV.8.58.2 nevertheless constitutes a discussion of the principles inherent in the verses *Gal.* 3.28 and *Col.* 3.11, and begins as follows:

> For the individual who is part of our polity can philosophise without learning, whether he be barbarian, Greek, slave, old man, boy, or woman. For self-control is common to all human beings who have chosen it. And we agree that the same nature and the same virtue exists in every race. And with regard to human nature, the woman does not possess one nature, while the man appears to have another, but they have the same nature and virtue.

Clement's thought here focuses on the two verses mentioned above, and he is concerned to stress equality of moral capacity between races and classes of people. The term virtue (*arete*) should be understood as meaning a moral skill or capacity, and it should be noted that Clement observes a difference between nature and moral capacity, since he mentions both on each occasion. He refers to an opinion that men are naturally prone to self-restraint and righteousness, and women to licentiousness and wrongdoing, but he greets this view with an explicit and flat rejection. The same nature produces the same virtue, though Clement wishes to classify this identical moral capacity as being of the soul. The natural differences between man and woman are emphasised, and it is claimed that the woman is made for child-bearing and housekeeping.

> As then there is sameness as regards the soul, she will attain to the same virtue. But since there is difference with regard to the specific characteristics of the body, she is made for child-bearing and housekeeping. 'For I wish you to know, says the apostle, that Christ is the head of every man, and man is the head of the woman'.
>
> (*Stromateis* IV.8.60.1; I *Cor.* 11.3)

In this way, couched in a traditional affirmation of New Testament patriarchal ideas, there is expressed an interpretation of the Pauline equality between classes, and between the sexes, which constitutes a departure from some of the harsher views of women taken by the Jews and some Christian encratic sects. Clement does make an unequivocal statement of the equality in moral capacity between men and women, without diverging from the principle of patriarchal authority.

Another passage (*Paedagogus* I.4.10.1) clearly has the *Galatians* 3.28 principle in mind, though it is not explicitly quoted: it is noted that there is one God for both men and women. Again Clement is more concerned with the annulment of difference, and does not attempt to draw out the social effects of sexual differentiation: it is characteristic of this world that we are separated into two sexes. In the next world we shall be 'removed from desire' and the need for marriage will be transcended: some hint of this new state is contained in the neuter word 'little child' which may apply to both girls and boys, and the Greek word for sheep has a similar usefulness. The Lord is in fact our shepherd, and we are his sheep. Clement is very much concerned with the overcoming of sexual differences, but he gives this a metaphysical significance which was no doubt distinctly inhibiting to any move towards social change. The overcoming of sexual polarisation, a familiar concern since Aristophanes' myth of primal androgyny, is the major focus of Clement's discussion, and almost certainly he sees the process of becoming 'as little children' (*Matt.* 18.3, see p. 78) as progress in this direction.

Other interpretations include a passage in the *Gospel of Philip* (49/Robinson 138), where the male/female distinction is omitted, but the other divisions are borrowed to make a special point. It is stated that if one claims to be a Jew, Roman, slave, freeman, no-one will find this remarkable, but if one claims to be a Christian the whole world will tremble. Hippolytus (*Ref.* 5.7.15), in his account of the Naassenes, reports on their hostility towards intercourse between man and woman. In their myth, Attis was emasculated, thereby passing from the earthly to the heavenly, where there is 'neither male nor female', but a new creature which is androgynous (*arsenothelus*). The Naassene interpretation of the principle thus envisages bisexuality, rather than asexuality, or the state of being neuter, as the higher spiritual goal. As Clement says in the *Paedagogus* I.6.31.1., 'all who have abandoned the desires of the flesh are equal and spiritual before the Lord', and there is here an allusion to *Galatians* 3.28, which is not listed in the *Biblia Patristica*, not being a quotation proper.

It is thus clear that the Christian interpretation of the Pauline principle envisaged no equality of role between men and women, so far as it has been pursued. The publication of further volumes in the *Biblia Patristica* would allow a further systematic treatment of the exegis of this particular verse, but it is fairly clear that at no stage did any branch of Christianity, whether orthodox or Gnostic, envisage a social application of this verse. The annulment of the male/female distinction is abstracted from the realities of day to day living and role distribution, and is construed as a statement of spiritual realities. That this is the Patristic interpretation of Paul's verse is of interest, though it does not tell us what Paul himself meant, since religious tradition makes its own rules for the interpretation of its sacred texts, and these rules derive from religious goals, rather than a concern with scientific exegesis. The Patristic interpretation of *Galatians* 3.28 is of importance insofar as it gives us an insight into the Patristic period.

Another verse whose history may be traced with interesting results is that which expresses the male/female relationship in its archetypal Western form, *Gen.* 3.16:

> To the woman he said, I will greatly multiply your sorrow and your conception; in sorrow you shall bring forth your children, and you shall desire your husband, and he shall rule over you.

There are many parts of the exegesis of the Adam/Eve story which could profitably be pursued as an exercise in the history of ideas, but this has been done by others (Higgins, Tavard) in certain respects. It is my intention here simply to deal with the later Christian interpretation of the last part of the curse, as pronounced on woman, namely that the husband shall henceforth dominate his wife, whose relationship to him will be one of yearning and subjection. A moment's reflection will reveal how important a place this notion has in our culture, since it captures the stereotype which has operated in the West since its very beginnings. This is not to say that Jewish culture has an absolutely rigid idea of love in the male/female relationship: the love poetry of the *Song of Solomon* has the woman yearning for and searching for the man. In the Authorized Version translation (3.1,2):

> By night on my bed I sought him whom my soul loveth: I sought him, but I found him not. I will rise now and go about in the city in the streets, and in the broad ways I will seek him whom my soul loveth: I sought him, but I found him not.
>
> Tell me, o thou whom my soul loveth, where thou feedest, where thou makest thy flock to rest at noon: for why should I be as one that turneth aside by the flocks of thy companions? (1.7)

But the same poetry knows how to reverse the Genesis principle of the woman's yearning for the man in the explicit variation of 7.10:

> I am my beloved's, and his desire is toward me.

The Gnostic interpretation of 3.16 integrates it into various myths, giving the Genesis view of women under the curse a new use in explaining the relationships of the various cosmic principles to each other. The *Hypostasis of the Archons* (27, 30/Robinson 159) uses it to explain the relationship of the mythical personage Norea to the Rulers of Darkness. Norea denies that they knew her mother Eve, claiming rather that they knew another woman. The arrogant Ruler replies that she must render service, as did her mother Eve. Similarly in the *Exegesis on the Soul* (79, 9/Robinson 184), the soul's voyage leads her to be united with her husband, that is her real husband, and the document quotes what appears to be an amalgamation of verses:

> For the master of the woman is her husband.

Both the notion of servitude and sexual desire as the post-Fall female condition are used in the *Apocryphon of John* (Robinson 122). Aldabaoth is lord over the woman, and a little later the chief archon is said to have placed sexual desire in her 'who belongs to Adam'. The two elements of the female condition are separated here, in order to be used in different stages in the myth.

Irenaeus gives a different twist to the whole story (*Adv. Haer.* III.23.2), noting that as a result of the Fall, the earth was cursed. Irenaeus claims that Adam was not cursed personally, since the curse was not to remain in man, but the earth itself. The woman was punished with toil, the pain of childbirth, and servitude towards her husband. But Irenaeus stresses that the full power of the curse fell upon the Serpent, who was cursed above all the beasts of the earth. It is well worth noting that Irenaeus seeks to deny on two counts the gravity of the curse, first by removing its application to the 'earth', and secondly by emphasising the greater damnedness of the Serpent. Irenaeus omits the implantation of sexual desire in women, choosing only to stress the idea of subjection.

Tertullian's discussion in *On the Apparel of Women* will be examined in more detail later, but he quotes the verse without any interpretative material other than the question directed aggressively at women:

> And do you not know that you are each an Eve?
>
> (*De cultu feminarum* 1.1.1.)

Elsewhere Tertullian simply reiterates the principle that the woman should be obedient, thereby encompassing the content of two Biblical passages, 1 *Cor.* 14.34 and *Genesis* 3.16. He does not mention the affliction of desire, but limits himself to the aspect of servitude (*Against Marcion* V.8.11). Elsewhere in this same work (2.11.1) there is an interesting thought: Tertullian notes that until the Fall, woman had brought forth children under a blessing, namely the command to Increase and Multiply. Until the Fall, woman lived in this happy state of blessedness, but after the Fall she became 'a slave to her male partner'. Tertullian adds, interestingly, that she had been destined to be a help, and not a slave, to the male: the clear implication is that female servitude is part of the curse resulting from the Fall, and that this situation is abnormal, waiting to be remedied through the forgiveness of sins and the eschatological resolution of history. The Fall can often serve as a kind of measure whereby one can detect what is regarded as contingent, temporary, and lamentable in the human condition, and so it is here with Tertullian, who sees female servitude as just such an unfortunate but temporary consequence of the Fall. (He notes that the Marcionite would interpret such a condemnation as a case of cruelty, and he even seems to agree that the curse was extremely severe.) This fact places in a different light the apparently anti-female stance of Tertullian in the moral works discussed later, and whilst it is true that he was responsible for some of the more resounding misogynist statements of ancient Christian writing, some of which have become famous, it seems that he saw this as a matter for regret, and as an inevitable consequence of the Fall. It would appear that Tertullian was a reluctant misogynist, forced into this position by his belief in the authority of the Genesis myth, though this might be to overestimate him.

One of the most interesting reflections on *Genesis* 3.16 may be found in Cyprian; *On the Dress of Virgins* 22. 'Hold fast, O virgins!' exclaims Cyprian, and argues that virginity compensates for all kinds of ills that might otherwise have been suffered, as a result of the curse. The virgin is free from the sentence of servitude to the husband, and from desire for him. The virgin's master is Christ, since she misses the intermediate stage of subjection to a male of the ordinary kind. A consequence of this is the remarkable claim that virgins are in all respects equal to men.

> You possess already in this world the glory of the resurrection. You pass through the world without the contagion of the world; in that you continue chaste and virgins, you are equal to the angels of God.

Thus virgins achieve equality not only with men, but also with angels. Now, one of the crucial questions of late antiquity concerns the growth of the cult of virginity, and its explanation; we are given in this passage of Cyprian a clear indication as to how the theological pressure applied itself in this direction. The curse of the Fall applied itself primarily to the *married* woman, and the virgin could escape both servitude to her husband, and desire for him. It may be seen that this technique of evading the consequences of the Fall is not quite legitimate, and that virginity is something of a clever evasion of what God had decreed to be the lot of women, but it is also true that there is ample precedent for Cyprian's view in Philo, for whom virginity was the first stage in becoming male. This maleness is a stage closer to the higher form of being, and virginity was a close approximation of it. The first chapter has dealt with this issue in Philo, but it can be noted here that there is a considerable posterity to the ideas adumbrated by this Alexandrian writer. The virgin escapes from the sentence of womanhood, and thus the ascetic life constituted a powerful impulse towards the belief that one was liberating oneself from the shackles which came with ordinary, standard womanhood.

The *Paedagogus,* or *Instructor,* of Clement of Alexandria contains much that is useful for the social history of Alexandria in that period of the early Roman Empire in which Alexandria was an intellectual and artistic capital. Book II, chapters seven and following reveal much of the lives of the wealthy and cultivated in Clement's own time and social class: chapter eight is devoted to the use of ointments and crowns, and is close in intention to some of Tertullian's works, to be discussed shortly, and which combine a moral system with specific instructions to women on dress and behaviour. Clement's passage is directed to both men and women, and is based on the idea that the use of crowns and ointments leads towards pleasures and indulgence, 'especially on the approach of night'. The anointing of Jesus' feet by a woman (*Matt.* 26.7) constitutes an apparent precedent which must be explained away, and the oil becomes the Lord himself, whereas the ointment is identified as Judas. Allegory thus prevents the New Testament from providing a precedent for the use of oils and unguents. Clement lists a considerable number of different types of oils which were popular, including the Plangonian and the Psagdian from Egypt, the Brenthian and the Metallian. Clement is referring to both men and women in this matter, and considers that the use of perfumes renders men effeminate. He refers to ointments made from roses, and powders which may be sprinkled on the clothes: men and women were apparently devoting endless energy to multiplying the fragrances which they could apply to themselves. It is better for women to breathe the genuine royal odour of Christ (there was a kind of deodorant called the 'royal', thus enabling Clement to make this pun). Nevertheless Clement is not absolutely opposed to the use of oils, and advises women to select a few sweet-smelling unguents, but not such as to overpower their husbands. Sweet scents have as their purpose the excitation of lust and this is the reason for moderating their use.

Clement describes a class of women (*Paed.* III.4) who are obviously idle and wealthy, and who are attended by eunuchs. Celts were responsible for carrying these women in their litters, and this mode of transport through the streets was part of the contemporary show of luxuriousness. Mention is made of the gullibility and impressionable nature of such women, and the way they are prevailed upon by people who win their confidence. Being carried through the streets, and purchasing bearers, would have been acceptable to Clement if modesty and the desire to be transported under cover had been the real motive for the practice, but in fact the women thus transported give the lie to this idea by peering and leaning out of their litters, gazing at the passing show. The women were often carried to the temples, where they devoted much time to religious practices, including sacrifices and soothsaying. These temples must have been places where procurers functioned, establishing relationships between the men and women who went there for just this purpose. These women took pleasure in frequenting androgynes; crowds of such bisexual men and generally 'abominable creatures' flocked to such places. Clement speaks of noises suggesting lust and sexual desire, the striking of suggestive poses, and most mysteriously, the habit of such people to make a noise through their noses resembling the croak of a frog. It is hard to guess at the significance of this particular practice.

Such women go to the baths and appear naked (III.5), even though at home they may be reluctant to appear naked before their husbands. Surrounded by effeminate (*anandron*) men, who have been dominated by women, they sit beside the baths eating and drinking from elegant gold and silver vessels. Women of this class tend to wash before their slaves, and allow their slaves to wash them. The mutual sexual enjoyment of this procedure is disguised by the fact that it had become an established custom. In contrast to this picture of Alexandrian womanhood, Clement quotes Zeno the Cittaean on the model for the ideal statue of a young woman (*Paed*. III.11.74.3):

> Let her face be pure, her eyebrows not bend downwards, nor her eyelids opened or turned back. Her neck should not be stretched back, nor should her limbs hang loose, but they should appear tightly-strung. She should have the sharpness of a right-thinking mind for discourse, and the ability to retain things spoken rightly. Her attitudes and movements should give no ground for hope to the licentious. She should display modesty and firmness.

Here is drawn for us the contrast between the ideal as Clement saw it, and the woman he observed in Alexandria. The languor and indolence associated with the baths, with oil massages, and overeating and overdrinking, is contrasted with tension of limb and mind. The ideal maiden is to be taut and firm in all aspects of her being. In contrast to the 'ogling eyes' and 'languishing looks' of the licentious, she should keep her eyes closed to a proper degree, with her eyebrows appropriately raised (*Paed*. III. 11.70.1). Opening one's eyes wide, and casting them upwards was seen to be a sign of sexual desire and availability. Clement speaks of the effeminate king of the Assyrians, Sardanapalus, and his casting up the whites of his eyes. All this means that the eye posture of the modest young maiden is particularly important, and it explains a great deal of talk about the downward cast of the eyes among the ancient moralists.

Tertullian has a number of treatises directed to moral issues and feminine behaviour. *On the Apparel of Women* is prefaced by a reminder to women that the first sin, that perpetrated by Eve, is a constant factor in the female condition, and that it must be expiated by an attitude of penitence. The woman must affect meanness of appearance, and go about humbly dressed. The Eve story, as the Fathers saw, could yield a variety of interpretations about the relative guilt of man and woman in the Fall, but Tertullian's was uncompromisingly condemnatory of women. He explicitly argues that the guilt incurred then, lives perennially and attaches to every woman in history.

> The sentence of God on your sex lives in this age; the guilt must necessarily live too!
>
> (*On the Apparel of Women*)

The principle of a timeless guilt is thus established, through using the typology provided by the Adam and Eve story to apply to the generalised human condition. Then follows:

> You are the devil's gateway; you are the revealer of that tree; you are the first deserter of the divine law; you are she who persuaded him whom the devil was not valiant enough to attack. You destroyed so easily God's image, man.

In what follows woman is also made responsible for Jesus' death, in that she had introduced the sin which made some compensation necessary, and this is of course close to a Christian anti-Semitic theme, with the difference here that responsibility for the death of God is laid at the door of women, rather than Jews. The first clause of the above passage has become famous as an indication of Tertullian's attitude to woman, and it is indeed a misogynist interpretation of the Genesis story which is being offered. It is worth noting that this tendency is a deeply rooted one, since Tertullian even has a reply ready for the person who asks why the serpent approached the woman only: he did not dare approach and tempt man, yet such was Eve's culpability that he was able to do so. All the finery sought by women, such as Tyrian dyed cloths, Milesian wool, pearls, jewellery, constitutes nothing more than the decor of her funeral celebration, since she stands condemned and in the state of death.

Female attire is divided into two categories (chap.4), involving the idea of clothing, and secondly ornamentation, such as care of the skin, the wearing of jewellery, but both of these are condemned, the one as a sign of ambition, and the other of prostitution. Then follows an elaborate discussion of gold and silver, and whether they are in any way superior to other metals, complaining that they serve no useful purpose like iron and brass. It is their rarity which makes them sought after for the purposes of personal decoration. Interestingly from the economic historian's point of view, Tertullian refers to the 'insane plenteousness' (*demens copia*) of gold and silver, while at the same time attempting to make an argument for their rarity. The treatment of colour is also interesting: Tertullian points out (I.8) that God would have created sheep with blue and purple fleeces had he wished people to wear clothes of this colour. Since such things do not spring from the hand of the author of nature, they must derive from its corrupter, namely the Devil. A similar argument is used against facial cosmetics: those who redden their cheeks and outline their eyes with antimony sin against God, because they are implying that his creative powers were inadequate (II.5).

Dyeing the hair with saffron is also to be disapproved of: such women would prefer to appear like Germans or Gauls, seeking after the red hair which was not common in Tertullian's North Africa. In replying to the Lord, who had spoken of the impossibility of making a black hair white, or conversely, they assert: 'we make it yellow'! (I.6). Dressing the hair in curls, or allowing it to flow loose is equally condemned: the use of wigs is also attacked. Men are not exempted from such attacks, and contemporary forms of male coquetry are condemned. Cutting one's beard too sharply (II.8), shaving around the mouth and removing body hair, fixing the hair with pigment and smoothing the body with powder, vain consultation of the mirror — all these habits are to be curtailed. Returning to women (II.4), Tertullian rejects the argument that women ought to be allowed to practise coquetry because they must please their husbands. He replies:

> Be without care, blessed sisters: no wife is ugly to her husband. She pleased him sufficiently when she was chosen, whether on the basis of character or form. Let none of you think that you will incur the hatred and repugnance of your husbands, if you refrain from caring for your appearance.

A believing husband does not require beauty, but chastity. It is true that a gentile husband might seek something more than chastity, but he will be prone to suspicion of his wife's activities. Tertullian's triumphant conclusion is that either way a woman is caught in the obligation not to be preoccupied with self-decoration, since in the one case the husband is not interested in her looks, and in the other case he is already suspicious, and should not be encouraged in this. It is interesting to note that this author is encouraging women away from the idea that they exist as attractive objects for men, having the responsibility of arousing male sexual desire by the various techniques listed above. It scarcely needs pointing out, however, that Tertullian's concern is not based on a desire for a greater degree of reciprocity in male/female relations, as a modern perspective might have it, but on the general need for keeping down the level of lust in the community. The essence of this advice to women is that too many attempts have been to interfere with nature in respect of matters of dress, and that self-decoration can only be for the purpose of exciting sexual desire, which was an undesirable result given Tertullian's ascetic outlook on moral matters. His own ironic style puts it well:

> It had escaped Him, when He was commanding the universe to come into being, to issue a command for the birth of purple and scarlet sheep! (II.10).

The writing *On the Veiling of Virgins* contains much interesting information. It appears that the churches in Greece kept their virgins veiled, and we are told that this sometimes happened in Africa: the variety of practice is of concern to Tertullian, since some women were advocating an end to the practice (3), and claimed to be 'scandalised' by it. His reply is that a change in church practice, which would force virgins to unveil themselves in the churches would be greeted with great hostility, and treated as a form of rape:

> You have denuded a maiden in respect of her head, and she ceases entirely to be a virgin in her own eyes: she has been made otherwise (3).

If Tertullian's evidence can be accepted, the practice had become a focal point of contention, and many women had internalised the restraint imposed upon them: thus a change in custom would inevitably cause a severe loss of self-esteem. The question is raised of why male virgins should do nothing to display their state, as women are obliged to do (10). Why should so many voluntary eunuchs carry their glory in secret, asks Tertullian, and makes some facetious suggestions, along the lines of wearing feathers, curls or using a British tattoo to indicate one's state and the pride one took in it. The men might simply wear veils as well, he further suggests, and notes that the more sexually attracted towards females one is, the more recognition might be given to one by the Holy Spirit. But this is in fact not the case, and Tertullian's sarcasm simply sidesteps the issue until the last sentence in the chapter.

> If nothing has been given to the male, much more has been given to the female.

This cryptic remark is preceded by the suggestion that man is closer to God, through being in his image, and I believe the line quoted means that this greater intimacy between God and the male is now compensated for by the gift of advertising one's virginity, given to the woman through the practice of wearing a veil. It is clear that there was a kind of spiritual pride abroad, over one's achievements in the suppression of sexual instincts, and it would be interesting to know more of the motives of two of the other parties in this discussion. In the first place, what were the views of the women who were scandalised by the practice of veiling virgins, and in the second, what were the views of the men who, far from objecting to the practice, actually sought to emulate it by wearing German curls, British tattoos and the like, at least according to the satire of Tertullian?

Some of his polemic against the Gnostic Marcion shows Tertullian in a more moderate light than his opponent, particularly as regards his attitude to the female body. Marcion objected to the idea of the incarnation of God in Christ, because it entailed Jesus' passing through the foulness of the female womb. Tertullian's account of Marcion's view is ironic, as ever, but the thrust of Marcion's view can be seen through his reporter's caricature:

> Come now, beginning from the nativity itself, declaim against the uncleanness of the genital elements in the womb, the filthy coagulation of fluid and blood, of the growth of the flesh for nine months out of that very slime. Describe the womb as it enlarges daily, heavy, anxious, not in repose even in sleep, uncertain in its likes and dislikes.

(*On the Flesh of Christ* 4)

The view that the womb and the female genitalia were disgusting was not an uncommon observation in the period, and it may be found in the non-Christian writer Celsus (Origen, *Contra Celsum* VI.73). In fact this opponent of Christianity used exactly Marcion's argument against the incarnation: God would surely have been able to reproduce himself without passing through the pollution of the female womb. It is for this reason, claims Celsus, that the idea of the incarnation is received with such incredulity, and had the idea of female procreation not been present, this aspect of Christian doctrine would have been so much the more acceptable. Origen's Christian reply is found in the same chapter, and is based on the analogy of a ray of sun, which itself remains pure and undefiled, even when it comes to rest on a dung-heap. Thus Origen implicitly recognizes the idea that there is something foul about the female reproductive organs, and does not take issue with his opponent on this point.

The view of the womb attributed to Marcion, as restless, troublesome and unstable finds precedent in the *Timaeus* (91C), where Plato speaks of the womb as if it has a life and will of its own, and describes it as 'a living creature desirous of child-bearing', which if it is frustrated of its goals, becomes vexed and causes all sorts of illnesses, creating great anxiety in the woman. This is the origin of the idea of hysteria, as a specifically female complaint, springing from the womb (*hystera*), which is seen as a destabilising element in the female body.

Unlike Origen, Tertullian does choose to fight on the issue of whether the female reproductive organs are innately disgusting, and in this chapter claims that God has redeemed human flesh. He loved not only man, but also his own birth and his own flesh:

> Take away the birth, and then show us the man; remove the flesh, and show us him who has been redeemed (4.5).

Thus Tertullian's theology provides for the endorsement and redemption of the flesh, including the female womb, and he develops this in chapters 19 and 20, where he provides some physiological material on his understanding of the generation process. As milk congeals into cheese, so the sperm congeals in a woman's blood: it is denied that this process followed sexual intercourse since the virgin birth is being maintained, but in other respects the natural process of coagulation occurred. Tertullian argues that the womb must have been functioning normally, since only in this case are the breasts activated (20), and changes in the womb can be the only explanation of their providing milk. This North African author is clearly more willing to accept the flesh and wombs, than the Alexandrians.

Origen, an Alexandrian writer of the third/fourth centuries, also lets us see how his opponent Celsus viewed woman in relation to the expanding Christian movement, thus giving glimpses of a pagan view of proselytised woman. In one passage (*Contra Celsum* III.4) Celsus claims that Christianity is attractive only to the gullible, and combines woman, slaves and children as a class of people who are particularly impressionable. Christians are only able to sway 'the silly, the mean and the stupid, with woman and children'. Origen does not reply directly to this in discussion (he has a habit of conceding implicitly a large number of points), though he reverts to it in III.49 and admits that the Gospel does invite the unintelligent, slaves, women and children, as well as the intelligent. Origen shows no desire to controvert a contemporary view of women. In II.59 Celsus attacks the credibility of the resurrection appearances, since the only witness was an hysterical female, Mary Magdalene and in II.70 the charge that the only witness was a woman is repeated. Origen's own view of what Christianity offers to women is given in III.56, where women are said to be turned away from a dissolute life, and from disputes with the people they live with, and from mad desire for theatre, dancing, and superstition. In III.10 he reflects on the power of the Christian gospel, since it made women forget the weakness of their sex, and follow their teacher into desert places.

Origen and Celsus have a social perspective which is rather similar, even though they are divided on the issue of Christianity. Both subscribe to the contemporary view of woman as flighty and naturally inferior to man. There is however one important difference between them, and that is that whereas Celsus is inclined to dismiss women, Origen adheres to a religion which at the outset shook women out of their customary subjection, and retained within its tradition stories concerning the acceptance of women, whether the woman of Samaria, or Mary Magdalene. Origen does not seek to take issue over Celsus' view of women, but takes issue over the idea that the religion should not receive and accept women.

Rosemary Ruether (*Misogynism and Virginal Feminism in the Fathers of the Church*) has argued interestingly that the emphasis on virginity derives from a monistic tendency in later Christian thought, whereby maleness was identified with monism, or singleness, and whereby femaleness was regarded as a secondary quality. An alternative approach was to characterize God by a nonsexual monism, transcending androgyny (154). The word *monos* means alone, or single, and it is the word from which 'monk' and 'monastic' derive (however see E.A. Judge, *The Earliest Use of Monachos...*): the celibate state was therefore intended to reach aloneness, and a Greek philosophical preoccupation with unity and multiplicity was grafted onto this enterprise. Duality was to be eschewed, and singleness became the goal. Ruether is concerned to distinguish between Christian writers who opted for characterizing the singleness of God as male (Augustine), and those who presented it as a unity lying beyond sexual imagery (Gregory of Nyssa). This is an important distinction, and it results from the greater theological conservatism of Augustine, as against the Platonic transcendentalism of Gregory of Nyssa. Augustine's belief in the power of ordinary language to capture theological ideas causes him to employ the imagery of human sexual experience to create a theological picture, with the result that true maleness in Adam is that which is in God's image. In the *Confessions* (13.32) Augustine praises God for the creation of the world, including man, made in God's image and likeness. Two forces are distinguished in man, that which deliberates and dominates, and that which is subject to such guidance. In the same way 'woman has been made for man'. She is subject to him, as our bodies are subject to our minds. There is no mistaking the inferiority of the female aspect, since in the *On the Lord's Sermon on the Mount* (29) the good Christian is portrayed as one who will hate the physical aspect of his wife, including anything to do with sexual intercourse, whilst loving the transformable part of her. It is strange that this view of the relative male/female qualities contrasts so greatly with the facts of Augustine's own family life, revealed in the *Confessions* 9.9. It was his father who was unfaithful rather than his mother, and his mother who showed the virtues of forbearance and patience. It was his father who was prone to emotion: he had a violent temper, and it fell to Monica to forbear and pacify him. She used to urge other women, whose faces were marked with the blows of their husbands, to hold their tongues, and recall their state of subjection to their husbands. Whilst the author of this book would have preferred that they respond to their husbands with karate rather than charity, it is fascinating to note the combination of ideal and practice in this issue.

It is often the case that the images and ideals thrown up by a culture seem to contrast oddly with actual social practice. The fourteenth century saw the flowering of the chivalric ideal, but also saw it juxtaposed with treachery, betrayal and ignobility: the Pope practised charity within earshot of the screams of tortured cardinals. The precise relationship of the ideal to the practice is a matter of some difficulty: it is not simply that the inhabitants of the fourteenth century were lying about their ideals, or that they were lying about their attempts to practise them, since it is also true that they did attempt in various ways to bring their ideals into their practice. (Social science attempts to deal with this problem through consistency theory, and on occasion such gaps between ideals and practice are referred to under the heading of 'cognitive dissonance', which refers to a state of post-decision conflict about the rightness of one's decisions. Such conflict is caused by gaps between theory and practice.) With respect to social history, two points must be made: firstly, it is obvious that cultural ideals should not be taken as clear guides to cultural practice, since these gaps do occur; but secondly, that such ideals must have some validity as indicators of social practice, since they constitute part of the group of environmental influences which cause behaviour. This second issue, of how to deploy cultural ideals as evidence for social history, is a complex one which goes beyond the scope of the present inquiry, but is clear that they must somehow be used.

To return to the case of Augustine's parents, we have noted the reversal of roles which had occurred: Monica seems to have been emotionally in control, and spiritually superior, in contrast to the typology laid down by the myth of Adam and Eve. An interesting interplay between the model and existing realities occurs in this passage of the *Confessions* (9.9). Monica advises her female friends, whose faces bear the marks of their husbands' attentions, not to gossip together about the evil nature of their menfolk, but to remember their condition:

> ...She humorously, yet gravely, advised them that since they had heard read the so-called matrimonial tables, they should regard them as contracts whereby they were made servants: thence they should remember their condition, and not defy their masters.

The Eve model is invoked in this way for the purpose of modifying the female self-image and female behaviour. The difficulty is that the Eve model is also supposed to provide an explanation for the female nature: it should not have been necessary for the model to be invoked, since the Fall ought to have resulted in natural female subjection. (Rosemary Ruether comments on this, 160 ff.) It is clear that we have here a case of the misleading model mentioned earlier. Eve's condition of servitude and desire is presented as an explanation of the nature of contemporary womanhood, but when reality is actually confronted, the explanation proves to be deficient, and becomes a model for behaviour, with a view to *making* the explanation appropriate to the facts. Part of the explanation of this is that a model is always inadequate in the area of ethics, and it is its very inadequacy which gives it its cogency. A life lived in approximate accord with a model of behaviour is the best stimulus towards a more accomplished representation of the model which is held out to the disciple.

Another example of the way Augustine applies the Eve model to apparently recalcitrant experience is found in *Confessions* 5.8, where Augustine describes the way in which he escaped from the dominance of his mother. As the astonishing tale has it, he loathed Carthage and wished to go to Rome; his mother wept bitterly and followed him to the water's edge, pleading with him to stay or take her with him. He managed to persuade her to spend the night praying in the shrine of Cyprian, and sailed away during the night, having deceived her as to his intentions. In Watts' translation (Loeb edition):

> The wind blew fair, and swelled our sails, and the shore withdrew itself from our sight. There on the morrow she fell into an extreme passion of sorrow, and with complaints and lamentations she even filled thine ears, which did for that little seem to regard them: when through the strength of mine own desires, then didst hurry me away, that thou mightest at once put an end to these same desires: and that her carnal affection towards me might be justly punished by the scourge of sorrows.

The extraordinarily intense relationship with his mother is thus briefly ruptured, and as a result she is plunged into paroxysms of grief. She did not know that Augustine's departure would in fact be a good thing for him (on her terms), so her torment was very great, and in this, says Augustine, she was demonstrated to have inherited the legacy of Eve. 'In sorrow she sought what she had brought forth in sorrow'. In this way he takes an ordinary aspect of female experience, and renders it comprehensible by reference to Eve's condition. It should be noted also that like Sophia in the Gnostic myth, Monica's problem was lack of knowledge: she did not know that Augustine's departure to Rome would result in his conversion, and so wept for nothing. Weeping, however, was her lot, and so she suffered an agony engendered by ignorance.

Augustine's view of woman is dominated by the idea of the curse, and particularly by the idea of woman as the pleasure principle. He refers to the idea (*City of God* 14.24) that men have will-power over most parts of their body, such as the arms or lungs, but they do not have power of control over the erection of the penis. The control of will is very important to Augustine (see 14.26), and he regards this as being the essence of what was lost after the Fall. The Paradisal state involves physical relations between man and woman which are subject to the control of will. In such a state, sexual relations would be based on need, and no penetration of the vagina would be necessary for fertilisation. Indeed, in the absence of lust, there would be no impulse to destroy the wholeness of the female organ. Augustine's hostility towards the erect penis is well-known, and constitutes an interesting indicator of the sexual attitudes of his society. He was clearly not alone in this, and one cannot help thinking of Tertullian's male virgins, proudly bearing tattoos as the sign of victory over their virile member. His point is however worth considering, because it is fundamental. The fact that some parts of the body appear to be controlled by will, whilst others are not, is interesting enough as a starting-point, and the obvious next step is that the penis, if not controlled by will, must be subject to something else. It is in fact woman which controls its tumescence, and responsibility for the erection is removed from its owner. Consequently it escapes his control, and escapes the rule of will and reason; consequently responsibility for it is lodged with womanhood. (Augustine's philosophy of human relations treats heterosexual relations as normative.) The whole area of sexual desire is thus firmly planted in the female domain, and from this springs the phenomenon of projection which may be noticed repeatedly in the Patristic writers, whereby men disown their own sexual desires, and attribute responsibility for them to the actions of women. The penis is an instrument which belongs more to women, than to the men to which it is attached.

The idea of the female object arises from the tendency of men, particularly in sexual matters, to use women for their own purposes and satisfaction, without regard to the purposes of the women involved. Augustine is not therefore the prime mover in establishing the female as object (see Rosemary Ruether 163), but he does a great deal to establish the male as object, since he defines sensuality as the primary drive of women. Sexual intercourse will therefore correspond, in Augustine's thinking, to the fundamental purposes of women in human relations, and it is women who will be most satisfied by marriage, since their sensuality makes them greatly in need of it. If marriage is defined as a remedy against lust, then a woman will have a great deal to gain, since she will obtain release from desire. In Patristic thought, desire and its resolution are female concerns, and on this view it is the male who runs the risk of becoming the object, since resolution of her desire is the specific demand made by him by woman. So it was with Sophia, who waited on Christ for the resolution of her passion.

The Pauline/Augustinian understanding of marriage as a remedy against concupiscence is not primarily responsible for the idea of the female as object, though it may well be responsible for encouraging the idea of the person as object, in sexual matters at least. In the first place such a formula encourages either party to use the other for virtually masturbatory purposes, but it is important to note, secondly, that this applies to the sexual sphere only. In other areas the Christian understanding of marriage involves respect for the needs of the other partner as a desiring subject: the difficulty arises simply because Christianity does not cater for sexuality as part of the pattern of reciprocity and recognition of self-hood. The real offender against the status of womanhood is not this definition of marriage, which only applies to the sexual side, and may create both male and female objects, but the definition of woman as being in subjection to man. The idea is far broader, far more dominant, and far more capable of permeating the whole status of women in society.

It is very important to stress the desire of women to escape the consequences of the curse, particularly those relating to subjection and desire. It is worthy of note that man could not escape the toil that now characterised his relationship to the earth, but that woman could escape child-bearing, subjection to and desire for a man, by escaping marriage. This became one of the most powerful impulses towards virginity, bolstered by the strong suspicion of sexuality which characterised the age. A passage of Cyprian has already been cited, indicating that virgins were seen to escape some of the consequences of the curse, by attaining a relative freedom while on earth. Gregory of Nyssa also dwells on how woman may escape from the perils and tensions of child-bearing (*On Virginity* 3): he notes that women often die in childbirth, and paints a gloomy picture of servants moving into the bridal-chamber to deck it out for mourning, and to prepare it for their wailing rites. Even if, he continues still more gloomily, the child and the mother both live, the fears attendant on the risks of accident or illness of the male are such as to make marriage a torment.

> But the oracle of God tells us that she is not her own mistress, but finds her resources only in him whom wedlock has made her lord; and so, if she be for ever so short a time left alone, she feels as if she were separated from her head, and can ill bear it; she even takes this short absence of her husband to be the prelude to her widowhood; her fear makes her at once give up all hope; accordingly her eyes, filled with terrified suspense, are always fixed upon the door; her ears are always busied with what others are whispering; her heart, stung with her fears, is well-nigh bursting even before any bad news has arrived...
>
> (*On Virginity* 3, trans. The Nicene and Post-Nicene fathers, ed. Schaff and Ware).

All this and more can be avoided through virginity, a remedy against the state laid down for women in *Genesis*, God's 'oracle'. However, Gregory does expand the concept to embrace male virginity as well, and the state in question becomes a stage of realised eschatology. The justification for men and women attempting to escape the consequences of the curse lies in their redemption, partially realised on earth. The cultivation of asexuality is a step in this direction, and chapter 5 tells us that the object of virginity is to prevent the soul being drawn downwards by outbreaks of sensuality. Virginity is the way up to Paradise out of this world 'which lieth in the Evil' (ch. 12), that Paradise which Paul perceived in the mystical experience described in 2 *Cor.* 12.4.

The two verses chosen earlier for particular study find reinterpretation in this treatise of Gregory of Nyssa. *Genesis* 3.16 figures in the passage quoted, and *Galatians* 3.28 finds a new meaning at the end of chapter 20. Gregory speaks of a spiritual marriage in which there is neither male nor female, and asserts that both men and women ought to aspire to this. Attached to his idea of a spiritual and asexual union stands the social phenomenon of spiritual marriages between monks and female Christian ascetics, the *virgines subintroductae* denounced by Jerome and John Chrysostom. Elizabeth Clark gives a careful review of this question, and locates with precision the views of Chrysostom on the question: 'From his point of view, the *subintroductae* and the monks had prematurely assumed that they had shed their bodily desires. Chrysostom, less given to illusions of heavenly incorporation, felt obliged to remind them that they were still of the earth, earthy' (185).

Jerome's thinly disguised prurience denounces the plague of 'beloved ones' (*agapetai*) who filled the church (*Letter* 22.14).

> Whence come these unwedded wives, these novel concubines, these harlots, so I will call them, though they cling to a single partner.

Jerome complains of their tendency to share beds, and even to have children, and it is clear that the state of spiritualised asexuality was often imperfectly achieved. *Galatians* 3.28 was understood as an immediate offer of asexuality, and combined with an interpretation of the curse of *Genesis* 3.14 ff. as a stage which could here and now be neutralised, its interpretation led to the growth of droves of failed virgins, cohabiting in failed spiritual marriages. Christians are prone to being hasty over eschatological matters.

Bibliography

Biblia Patristica. A list of Biblical citations in the Church Fathers, vols. 1-2, Centre National de la Recherche Scientifique, Paris 1975 and 1977. Vol. 3 appeared in 1981, too late for use.

Gospel of Thomas. See J.M. Robinson (ed.), chapter 2.

Clement of Rome. See Apostolic Fathers (Loeb Classical Library edn.) for English translation.

Clement of Alexandria, *Stromateis, Paedagogus* and *Protrepticus* may be consulted in English in the Ante-Nicene Christian Fathers series (vol. II): The Protrepticus has also appeared in the Loeb Classical Library edition.

Gospel of Philip. See J.M. Robinson (ed.)

Hippolytus, *Refutatio* (see chapter 2).

Higgins, J.M. *The Myth of Eve;* Journal of the American Academy of Religion 44 (1976) 639.

Tavard, G.H. *Woman in Christian Tradition* (University of Notre Dame Press 1973).

Hypostasis of the Archons. See J.M. Robinson (ed.)

Apocryphon of John as above.

Irenaeus, *Adv. Haer*. See chapter 2.

Tertullian *On the Apparel of Women; Against Marcion*. (May be consulted in English in the Ante-Nicene Library series, vols. 3 and 4).

Cyprian, *On the Dress of Virgins*. As above, vol. 5.

Tertullian, *On the Veiling of Virgins*. As above.

Origen, *Contra Celsum*. See *Origen. Contra Celsum,* by H.K. Chadwick (Cambridge 1965).

Plato, *Timaeus*. May be consulted in English in the Loeb Classical Library edition.

Ruether, Rosemary, Misogynism and Virginal Feminism in the Fathers of the Church, in *Religion and Sexism* (New York 1974).

Judge, E.A. *The Earliest use of Monachos for 'Monk' and the origins of Monasticism;* Jahrbuch für Antike und Christentum 20 (1977) 72-89.

Augustine, *Confessions, City of God*. In the *Basic Writings of Saint Augustine,* ed. Whitney J. Oates, 2 vols., Random House, New York, 1948; also in the Loeb Classical Library series. *On the Lord's Sermon on the Mount,* see Latin text in Migne, *Patrologia Latina* vol. 34.

Gregory of Nyssa, *On Virginity,* in The Nicene and Post-Nicene Fathers series, vol. 5.

Jerome, *Letters,* as above, vol. 6.

Clark, Elizabeth, *John Chrysostom and the Subintroductae;* Church History 46 (1977) 171-185.

See also

Clark, Elizabeth and Richardson H. *Women and Religion*. A Feminist sourcebook of Christian Thought (Harper and Row 1977).

Clark, Elizabeth, *Sexual Politics in the Writings of John Chrysostom,* Anglican Theological Review 1977.

Daniélou, J. *Nuns: what is special about them?* (London 1974) *The Ministry of Women in the Early Church* (London) Faith Press, 1961.

Ferrante, J.M. *Woman as Image in Medieval Literature* (New York 1975).

Morewedge, R.T. (Ed.) *The Role of Women in the Middle Ages* (State University of New York Press, Albany 1975).

Chapter Five

Woman in Islam

The founder of Islam, Muhammad, was born in Mecca in 570 A.D.: he had never known his father, and his mother died when he was six. He lived in Mecca for about forty years, in an environment little affected by Judaism or Christianity, and thus participated in the important pre-Islamic phase of Arabic culture. While still in Mecca he received his prophetic call, and began to preach his fiercely idealistic message, which contained elements of Judaism, Christianity and Hellenism. He had begun to associate himself with a group called the 'pure ones' (hunafa), whose notion of God was strictly monotheistic: Muhammad began to retreat to a cave on a mountain-top near the city, where he would meditate. Here, in a vision, he received a command: 'Recite!' In response to his reply: 'What shall I recite?' came the revelation of the first part of Koran 96 (or perhaps, 68, 74, 93). Despite great self-doubt, the reassurance of his wife and friends convinced him that he had in fact received a divine revelation, and he began to campaign against the religious establishment in Mecca. Muhammad considered himself the last of the prophets, and there is much in the early part of the Koran which is reminiscent of the morals and theologies of some Christian sects. It is possible to piece together an Islamic christology from the Koran, for example, and it does not constitute the total break with Christianised antiquity that some might imagine it to be. Given this connection with the development of Christian antiquity, and given the immense historical significance of Muhammad's prophetic experience, it is important to complete this study with some observation on the Islamic woman. Today every seventh person is a Muslim, and the Muslim dominates much of Asia, and south-east Asian areas such as Malaysia and Indonesia: approximately four hundred and fifty million followers testify to the historical significance of Muhammad's calling.

Problems concerning Jewish/Christian hermeneutic, or manner of interpreting the sacred books, have already been alluded to. The status of the Koran in the Islamic system of authority is somewhat different. Islam does not have the Christian distinction between revelation and inspiration, because the Koran is held to be the word of God himself, dictated directly to his prophet Muhammad, who simply transcribes it. There is therefore less room for reinterpretation or transmutation of the sacred text than there is in Christianity, and the sources of authority are even more rigidly defined than in Judaism or Christianity: thus the Koran occupies a place which is closer to that of Christ himself in Christianity, than to that of the Bible. It is the incarnate Word of God. This does not mean that varieties of interpretation are excluded, however, especially since philosophy develops throughout the whole period of Islamic history and is closely associated with Islamic religious sentiment. This parallel current of thought, together with Muslim mysticism, provided an alternative body of ideas which could be brought to bear on the interpretation of the Koran.

D.S. Margoliouth (*The Early Development of Moham-medanism*) notes that at the death of Muhammad there was no definitive text of the Koran established, and that a number of his companions claimed to know sufficiently great numbers of its passages by heart for a document to be established. Though the utmost importance was attached to the words of Muhammad, there is doubt over what they actually were and over how closely the Koran represents them: similarly for the words of Jesus, and their representation in the Gospels. In respect of the Koran, the earlier commentaries do no more than guess at the meanings of the Suras and do not claim to offer an infallible interpretation. Islam recognizes that each nation has its own book and Allah's task will be to confront the books of other peoples with the book of Islam. Allah was responsible for giving the Israelites their book and their commandments, but they began to disagree among themselves. This sectarianism will fall under the judgment of

Allah (Suras: 45.8; 45.16).

There is no clear set of moral commandments, though it is possible to deduce precepts by analysing the whole of the Koran. Some are historically determined, and thus moral principles may fluctuate according to circumstances: Margoliouth claims that the Fortieth Sura is determined in its tone ɔ warfare and by immigration, and is clearly addressed to those who might be wavering in their belief, stressing as it does the vast chasm which separates the believers from the non-believers, and the vengeance to come for those who follow another path. In the ninth Sura, the prophet comments on an actual battle (Hunain, dated to A.D. 630) between Muslims and Meccans, asserting that Allah's support was a crucial factor: Islamic theology often reacts to historical situations and the moral code finds its expression in response to them.

Thus the Koran is not, and does not include, a clearly codified set of rules of behaviour, to be used for defining the status of woman for example. As with Christianity, there grew up an oral tradition which supplemented and clarified the teachings of the Koran. It was important that this tradition remain oral, that it be memorised and passed from person to person in this manner. A written document commanded less authority, because it stood as a competitor to the Koran, which was considered to be the only, and complete, written document for Muslims. For these reasons, there developed a moral code and a body of doctrine outside the Koran, which could influence the way in which its authority was felt. Evolution within the Koran itself has already been noted, and in this can be instanced in the Sura devoted to woman (4). Margoliouth (78) notes that the punishment for adulteresses is more lenient in Sura 24 than in Sura 4, in the latter case the required punishment being imprisonment of the adulteress for life, whereas in the former a mere one hundred stripes is allocated (to both adulterer and adulteress). He argues that progress has occured, that Sura 24 is later than Sura 4, and concludes that the prophet has evolved towards leniency. It is further noted that whilst the Koran may prescribe these punishments, which show internal differences and change of opinion within the book, practice prescribes yet another sanction, which is harsher than either prescribed by the text: the adulteress must be stoned. In this way traditional Muslim practice proves itself to be harsher, and more prone to blame women for deviation from 'normal' sexual relations, than the commandments of the Koran.

In 1846 M. de Sokolnicki published in Paris a book entitled *Mahomet, législateur des femmes,* and this work is an interesting relic of the discussion of feminist issues and of Muslim culture, in the first half of the nineteenth century in Paris. (Oddly, the author adds an appendix on the view of Christ and Christians expressed in the Koran.) His intention is to defend Muhammad against the slanders of such writers as Montesquieu (8), who blame the former for the abject situation of the Muslim woman, and he attributes such slander to Christian malice and anti-Muslim prejudice. De Sokolnicki approves of the view, attributed to Montesquieu (*Esprit des lois* XIV, 2), that in cold climates there is little stimulus towards sexual pleasure, in temperate climates moderate sensitivity to sexual pleasure, and in hot climates a great deal of interest in the pleasures of the body. Muhammad had therefore to deal with the sexual passions of a hot climate, and thus ordained polygamy (or more exactly, polygyny), being of a realistic turn of mind. (One notes that on this view, Muhammad managed to cater successfully for the passions of the over-heated oriental male, whose four wives helped him deal with the climate, but that by the same token he achieved very little for the over-heated oriental female, unless he imagined her to be homosexual, which is doubtful). In the words of de Sokolnicki (11): 'He (i.e. Muhammad) knew only too well the stubborn resistance offered by (the desire for women) to anything which seeks to diminish its sway, and the extreme violence with which it destroys anything which dares to strike at its existence... We have only to recall all the atrocities, all the crimes, all the immorality caused by the imposition of monogamy in Goa and the Portuguese possessions of India.' Further, says de Sokolnicki, in terms which remind us of Marx, the Western system of marriage is in fact an ill-disguised form of polygamy: an unnamed but contemporary public figure is quoted as asserting that 'one whole area of Paris is nothing other than the harem of that great multiple sultan called the husband'. Such considerations lead the author to consider Muhammad's way of dealing with women to be more realistic and less hypocritical than that obtaining in the Western law and practice of his own time. He compares Oriental polygamy, when the husband acquires rights over several women, but also many duties towards them and their children, favourably with Western monogamy, where a man is obliged by law to protect only one woman and one set of children, and where the rights of mistresses and their children are left to his arbitrary discretion.

De Sokolnicki is however kindly disposed towards those seeking to assist women towards a better place in society, and deals with what must have been a contemporary issue over the right of women to be educated, quoting (21) without reference Fénélon: 'Mention is made of the weakness of women, but the weaker they are, the more important it is to strengthen them'. On the same theme, also without reference, the Abbé Fleury is quoted: 'It is held that women are not capable of education, as if their soul were of a different species from the male soul, as if they had no less than us, reason to be guided, will to be regulated, passions to be battled with, and as if it were easier for them than us to meet all those needs without learning anything!' The Author's discussion of Islam leads him to a contemporary debate as to the nature of woman. Strangely, however, the concern he manifests for the female class accompanies a defence of Arab polygamy and a defence of Muhammad's role in recognizing it and establishing it. Quoting Montesquieu again (*Esprit des lois* XVI, 2), he argues that women in hot climates are nubile at the age of eight, nine, or ten, and already old at thirty, having ceased to be fertile at twenty-eight. Marriage and childhood go together therefore, and it is claimed that the extremely short period of female usefulness in the hot climate naturally leads to polygamy. Muhammad, it is agreed, had the intelligence and practicality to recognize this, and to ally himself with nature. We have in this way the odd spectacle of a mid-nineteenth century writer referring with approval to the pro-feminist sentiments of French moralists and philosophers of the eighteenth century, yet defending with tremendous passion the institution of polygamy in Islam, on the basis of an allegedly empirical doctrine of the female nature in hot climates. De Sokolnicki does however denounce with fervour those slanderers of Muhammad who attribute to him the doctrine that the woman is worth less than the man, and that therefore a crime against a woman deserves lighter punishment than that same crime perpetrated against a man; it is also denied that Muhammad promulgated the idea that women may not enter mosques. Such ideas are attributable to the tradition which constructs itself around the Koran, but are not found in the teaching of Muhammad himself.

What does the Koran teach about women? One whole chapter is devoted to women, a fact which is interesting enough itself since there is no Sura devoted to men: one immediately suspects that Allah is more preoccupied with regulating the lives of women than men. Sura 4 occurs early in the traditional ordering of the Koran, but it is generally thought to have come late in the actual drafting of the document. There is, however, material scattered throughout the document on the various problems of managing womanhood, displaying a blend of commonsense and moral purism. Muhammad declares that Allah has not given man two hearts: his adopted son is not to be considered his real son, and should bear the name of his genuine father. Such ethical clear-headedness should also be brought to bear on the practice of divorcing one's wife without releasing her (33.4: reference is made here to the custom of declaring a wife to be in the same position as one's mother, thereby denying her sexual rights, but imprisoning her within the marriage). There is a sense here of the inappropriateness of double standards: 2.221 orders the Muslim not to marry an Unbelieving woman, recommending a Believing slave-woman in preference.

There are a great number of Koranic recommendations on caring for the interests of women within the generally polygamous structure of society envisaged. There is much down to earth financial advice, regulating ordinary patterns of behaviour to a much greater extent than Christian writings, for example: a 'dowry', in the sense of a pre-nuptial gift from the husband to the prospective wife is provided for. The Sura on women (4.3-4) suggests that the male marry women of his choice, up to four in number, and that the wife should receive her dower as a free gift on marriage. It is suggested that if the wife should return any of the dower to her husband as a gift, he should take it with good grace. If the wife is sexually unfaithful, the husband may retrieve part of the dower (4.19). Despite the fact that the powers of the husband seem to loom large in this regard, it is to be noted that custom expects him to provide his wives with a degree of financial independence. This is the importance of the dowry (or 'jointure', 'dower') in Islamic law, and the Iranian civil code under the Shah provides for such a dowry to be established by the prospective husband in favour of his wife. The sum is to be known by both parties in advance,and afterwards becomes the exclusive property of the wife, to be used as she wishes (article 1082, Code Civil iranien, ed. Aghababian). Another article (1085) provides for the possibility of the wife refusing to perform her marital duties if she has not received the dower promised. Inheritance and divorce settlement is covered in detail in the Koran. Sura 4.11 provides for the estate left to the male child to be double that left to the female child, and the practical effect of this would have been to ensure that the male role in society was reinforced, so that the individual man could assume the responsibility of maintaining women and providing dowers. Needless to say it also ensured that the female role, that of receiver and dependent, was also reinforced. In case of death, the widow was to be provided with a year's maintenance and housing (2.240): if, however, she should leave the residence during this year, no blame attaches to the male whatever he might do ('provided it is reasonable'.) If the wife dies, the husband may receive half of the estate (4.12), but if there is a child, the husband receives one quarter. Sura 2.241 recommends that for divorced women a reasonable amount of maintenance should be paid. In the case of Believing women who have fled from Unbelievers, financial arrangements are complicated. If it is clear that such women are in fact Believers they should be given refuge, and it should not be thought that Unbelievers are in any way legitimate husbands for them. Despite this, Unbelieving husbands should be reimbursed for their expenditure on the dower. Similarly, Unbelieving women should be returned to their society with a request for reimbursement of the dower, if such expenditure has been undertaken (50.10).

Divorce is carefully regulated from the male point of view. In case of difficulties within a marriage the prophet recommends that an arbiter should be appointed from the families of both parties to assist in the process of reconciliation (4.35). In the event of serious difficulties a form of temporary divorce is possible; if reconciliation occurs the tentative divorce is revoked. This type of divorce may occur twice, after which the parties must make up their minds to live together peacefully, or else separate on a mutually considerate basis (2.229). It is interesting to note that in certain cases it is permissible for the wife to give some material reward to the husband in return for her freedom. Sura 2.225-6 refers to the apparently rash Arab habit of making oaths on the spur of the moment, such as the oath to abstain from one's wife. If such an oath has been sworn, the husband must wait at least four months before he returns to his wife, but if he persists in his renunciation, divorce may follow. In this way the solemnity of the oath is preserved, but the husband is encouraged to resume his conjugal duties after a decent period has elapsed: Allah will let him off the hook, as it were, and indeed encourages him not to make the oath a pretext for failing to perform as required. Reference has already been made to the practice of separation through the fiction of declaring one's wife to be one's mother: in this case also Muhammad makes a critique of contemporary Arab practices, adopting a higher moral stance, and defending female rights, though within the general structure of patriarchal authority and polygamy (33.4: 58.2). Again, in the case of dower arrangements in case of divorce, he appears to be giving advice of a humane and common-sense sort which will have the effect of protecting the wife's position in this type of society. Sura 2.236 provides for divorce before the complete consummation of the marriage: if this occurs before the dower has been given, then a suitable gift should replace it. It the divorce occurs after the gift of the dower, half of it should be returned to the man (2.237). It is provisions like this which cast Muhammad in the light of a humane reformer, who may have had the moral edge over others of his time in the sphere of male/female relations: like Paul, he suffers from the imposition of a twentieth century perspective, and the true nature of his relationship to his contemporaries is obscured. In the abovementioned case, Muhammad suggests a code of behavior for the man: if the divorce occurs after the gift of the dower it is 'more proper that the husband should forgo his share' (2.237, Penguin translation).

Adultery is punished harshly and in a variety of ways. A higher moral code appears to be expected of free women than of slave women in this matter, since slave girls who have committed adultery suffer only half the penalty inflicted on a free woman

(4.25). Both the woman and the man guilty of adultery should be flogged with one hundred stripes, witnessed by a party of believers (24.2), and the firm intention to preserve the strength of the marriage bond is illustrated by the provision immediately following: adulterers may only marry adulterers, or Unbelievers. In this way a shamed class of deviants from the marriage norms of the society is intended to be created, and the loss of face and moral opprobrium consequent on marrying into such a class must have considerably reinforced the marriage institution.

Polygamous marriage, providing for up to four wives for a man must have diminished the urgency of adultery on the part of males, but tended to make women more prone to it, since the chances of their obtaining sexual satisfaction were lessened. It is to be expected in this situation that adultery may have been more frequently a female pursuit, and the savagery of the traditional punishment by stoning (a practice which grew up independently of Koranic influence) must signify the male riposte to the inherent instability of his harem. Sura 4.129 reflects this problem, seen from a male point of view, since it is observed that a man will never be able to treat all his wives impartially, with equal attention, no matter how much he wishes to do so: the pragmatic prophet advises however that a man should not ignore any of his wives completely, whilst recognizing that he will not be able to devote his fullest attention to all of them at once. The husband may receive any one of his wives according to his pleasure, taking them out of turn if he so wishes, and no blame attaches to him if he decides to receive a wife that he has set aside (this will satisfy both her and him, and so all parties will be happier than they would have been given an over-rigid observance of moral principles: Allah is most forbearing; 33.51).

The act of intercourse pollutes, and men must cleanse themselves by washing before prayer, not only after sexual intercourse, but also after illness, journeys or excretion. If one has had intercourse with women while travelling, and can find no water, one should perform a symbolic act of cleansing, rubbing face and hands with clean sand. The command is directed towards men, and it is not clear whether women are similarly polluted by intercourse, that is, whether it is the act which pollutes, or whether it is the female who constitutes the pollutant. Menstruation is considered to be unclean, and men must abstain from intercourse during this period, though they should resume afterwards as Allah has commanded (2.222). The Koran continues: 'Women are your fields: go, then, into your fields as you please' (2.223: Penguin translation, N.J. Dawood). In a popular commentary (the Abdullah Yusuf Ali edition, Lahore 1969), this is explained as follows: 'Sex is not a thing to be ashamed of, or to be treated lightly, or to be indulged to excess. It is as solemn a fact as any in life. It is compared to a husbandman's tilth: it is a serious affair to him: he sows the seed in order to reap the harvest. But he chooses his own time and mode of cultivation.'

There is a clear implication that the man is superior to woman. In 4.34 it is stated that Allah has given more strength to the male sex than the female, and men are said to be the protectors and maintainers of women. Consequently women are obedient. Men are tempted by numerous things, among them women and offspring (3.13). Yet among these women and children may be enemies, of whom one must beware (64.14).

Allah, in his exclusivity, does not forgive the sin of worshipping other gods, though other matters may be overlooked. It is remarkable that Unbelievers are identified by the fact that they pray to female gods, and that in this they stand condemned (4.117). Islamic women are commanded to preserve their modesty and to cover their adornments and their bosoms, concealing their finery except to a long and specific list of those in the family (or family circle) who may be permitted to perceive it, including slave-girls, eunuchs and young children. The Arab taste clearly runs to bashful virgins with high breasts, since that is what is laid up in paradise for the righteous, as well as gardens and vineyards (78.34). In 55.56 the maidens of paradise are said to be of modest gaze, and as yet untouched. The true servants of Allah will dwell with dark eyed virgins: many passages of the Koran refer to the 'houris', the wide-eyed virginal beauties laid up for the virtuous Muslim (37.47). In 38.52 mention is made of an abundance of food and drink in store for the righteous as well as the usual bashful virgins. There is no mention of the rewards a female may expect, in the way of corresponding ideals of masculinity.

In sum, the Koran is a man's book, written for men and from their point of view. This is not to say that its teaching is inhumane

A modern comment on an ancient myth: a wall in Glebe, Sydney.

or lacking in common-sense: this would be quite untrue, since its tone is in many cases reformist in character. Taken overall, the Koranic teaching on women is more directed to improving their lot than it is to exploiting it, and in many cases Muhammad addresses himself to problems of contemporary practice. He makes no revolution, but he does make reforms. In certain respects the Koranic teaching guarantees a certain degree of freedom and independence: the practice of the giving of a dower (the premarital gift from husband to prospective wife) allows the woman some power of financial management, which acts as a counterweight to the supreme power of sexual management which the husband possesses over his wives. The provisions of a modern Islamic legal code have already been noted in this regard, that of Imperial Iran, and it may be reiterated that article 1085 allows the wife to refuse to perform her marital duties if she has not in fact received the pre-nuptial gift. This particular legal system delineates in detail the duties of husband towards a wife: he must provide for the wife's keep, including food, lodging, clothing and furnishings appropriate to the woman's said station; servants must be provided if the wife's state of health or social background warrants it (article 1106). Yet the rights of the husband are those of a potentate: he may prevent his wife from working if this is detrimental to the interests of the family, to his wife's prestige, or to his own (article 1117). Similarly, the husband can divorce his wife when he wishes, simply by pronouncing the word 'Talagh' in the presence of two male witnesses (article 1133).

Family law has been reformed in many Muslim countries in recent years: in 1967 the Iranian legislature enacted a family protection law, dealing with divorce and polygamy. In consequence a man seeking to marry more than one wife had to seek the permission of the Court. He was to declare any existing wives, and if the first wife did not agree to the second marriage, she could seek to have her own marriage dissolved. The survey edited by Tahir Mahmood (see end of chapter) indicates similar changes in India and Indonesia, for example. In India, until the Dissolution of Muslim Marriages Act of 1939, it was impossible for a Muslim woman to obtain the dissolution of her marriage from a court, no matter to what neglect, abuse or maltreatment she may have been subjected. The polygamous marriage frequently produces a situation where a wife may cease to please, and may therefore be supplanted economically, emotionally and sexually. The 1939 Act lists a number of procedures to be followed with regard to the management of the dower, for example, but also grounds on which a Muslim woman may seek dissolution of her marriage, such as disappearance of the husband, his continued impotence, insanity, affliction with leprosy or venereal disease, failure to provide maintenance, or perform other marital obligations. Cases of cruel treatment may also be given as grounds, such as habitual assaults on the wife, forcing an immoral life on the wife, interfering with her property, or her religious practices, or such as inequitable treatment in the case of a plurality of wives. One recalls here the Koranic injunctions on dealing with each wife on an equal footing, and it can be observed that the Koran and contemporary Muslim law are in a much closer relationship than the Bible and contemporary family law in Western countries.

Islam was a twelfth century importation into Indonesia and consequently brought a critique of existing social institutions. In the field of divorce, however, existing practice gave the Indonesian husband more arbitrary power than did Islamic law: a husband's right to divorce his wife was unrestricted, and Islam did at least possess a number of precautionary and advisory precepts aimed at discouraging divorce and encouraging reconciliation. Dutch administration had attempted to deal with the problem, but after independence a thoroughgoing reform was enacted (in 1946), following which marriage officials were appointed across the country. The male seeking divorce has to apply to the marriage official, who is required to make a total of two attempts to reconcile the parties before divorce can take place. This legislation is directed to the problem of the arbitrary exercise of male powers, and not at all to the problem of how woman might seek to obtain a divorce, or to what rights she might be entitled.

Islam defines itself by its law. Although theology and philosophy have a long and impressive tradition within the Islamic world, it is rules of behaviour which have been the essential contribution of Muhammad to the world's manner of being. Islamic law is not however like Christian canon law, in that there is no supporting organism, like the Church, which sponsors and strengthens it. In the Christian tradition the Church developed out of a new race within the Roman Empire, the Christians, and became an organization which competed with the State. No such rivalry existed in the Islamic state, and consequently the rules of the sacred book, the Koran, have not constituted the battle-ground that Christian ethics have become. There is much closer relationship between Koranic ethics and the law of Islamic states than there is between Biblical ethics and the laws of the Christian West. In Islamic thought all acts are assessed from a moral standpoint. Schacht (*The Legacy of Islam,* 396) claims that Islamic law placed human actions in one of the following categories: obligatory, recommended, indifferent, reprehensible, forbidden. It is within this framework of ethical thought that the fourth Sura of the Koran, devoted to woman, must be understood. Here are laid down a series of principles for the management of women, and these principles are more or less binding depending on which of Schacht's categories (listed above) they fall into.

It was observed initially that the fact that one whole Sura of the Koran should be devoted to women is in itself remarkable. This mixture of recommendations, rules and prohibitions must surely point to an Arabic social problem at the time of the origins of Islam. Defenders of Islam often point to the reformist character of Muhammad's teaching, and to the over-supply of women in Arab countries at the time and previously, which meant that a humanely organised form of polygamy was necessary. There is rarely advanced any evidence or statistics for this great imbalance between the female and the male population. It is simply asserted, and it is clear that there needs to be a careful assessment of the question. Ameer Ali (*The Spirit of Islam* 222) begins his chapter on the status of women in Islam as follows: 'The frequent tribal wars and the consequent decimation of the male population, the numerical superiority of women, combined with the absolute power possessed by the chiefs, originated the custom which, in our advanced times, is justly regarded as an unendurable evil'. The Islamic conscience has altered to the extent that polygamy has become a matter for defence and self-condemnation; hence the change in Iranian law which requires court approval for a polygamous marriage.

This alleged imbalance causes some to defend Islamic

polygamy as a wise and humane way of caring for the excess female population, since women are thus included in a domestic unit where they may be housed, fed and clothed. Changing demographical patterns diminish the need for this institution, but it is probably true that it is more the impact of Western thought which has precipitated the tendency to regulate or forbid polygamy. Changes in the composition of the population would account for its falling into disuse, but not for the present tendency to denounce it and turn against it within the family of Islam. Such a development is but continuing the direction taken by Muhammad himself, since the teaching of the Koran is reformist in character. Sura 4.3 teaches that one may marry two, three or four wives, but if one fears that it will be impossible to treat them with equal fairness, then one should take only one wife. It is Muhammad himself who initiates the decline of Islamic polygamy, though it is also Muhammad who immobilises social progress at the stage of his own particular reforms.

Bibliography

The Koran, trans N. J. Dawood (Penguin Classics).

Ali, Ameer. The Spirit of Islam (Methuen 1967).

de Sokolnicki, M. Mahomet, législateur des Femmes (Paris 1846).

Gibb, H.A.R. &Kramers, J.H. The Shorter Encyclopedia of Islam (Leiden 1953).

Macdonald, D.B. The Development of Muslim Theology, Jurisprudence and Constitutional Theory (N.Y. 1903).

Mahmood, T. ed. Family Law Reform in the Muslim World (prepared under the auspices of the Indian Law Institute, New Delhi). Printed in Bombay, undated.

Margoliouth, D.S. The Early Development of Mohammedanism (N.Y. 1914).

Schacht, J. The Origins of Muhammadan Jurisprudence (Oxford 1974). The Legacy of Islam (Oxford 1974).

Conclusion

The portrait of Woman

The woman of the ancient world was immobilised into a stylised portrait whose lines have now become discernible. The Jewish/Christian tradition brings the story of Eve's enticement of Adam into evil, and the consequence of the curse laid upon mankind. The specific curse upon woman lies in the following words:

> I will greatly multiply your pain in childbearing; in pain you shall bring forth children, yet your desire shall be for your husband, and he shall rule over you. (*Genesis* 4.16)

This principle defines a role for women, and must be treated as a cause in social patterns of behaviour. We are not dealing here with a vague correlation between deities and institutional behaviour, but rather a normative image for female comportment. Christianity is a religion of traditional authority, and the Eve story provides a point of reference through which leaders in church matters could develop a doctrine of womanhood. Not only did men seek to channel behaviour into a pattern formed by these words, but women also endeavoured to conform to the model. Augustine's mother actually endeavours to make the model of servitude to her husband fit herself, and recalls her friends to the same principle (see 88): though she was in all respects stronger than her husband, she accepts a behavioural norm which controverts this. Augustine sees her distress and her outpourings of grief as a living out of the Genesis principle (89): it is woman's lot to grieve. May we surmise that the belief in the curse of painful child-bearing actually increased the pain of women in labour? Such ideas tend to enter into behaviour, thus becoming social fact.

A feature of the image of woman which is common to all the traditions which have been discussed is the equation of woman with desire, or passion. The Valentinian Sophia was characterised as being subject to fear, entreaty, distress and sorrow, and these passions constitute her until she is liberated from them by her lover, sent by Christ. This picture of woman is one of the most significant to be found in antiquity, since it seems to summarise, in mythical form, so much of the understanding of woman in the literature of late antiquity. If there is one single theme to be drawn out of the material reviewed thus far, it is that woman is seen as akin to passion, and subject to passion, whereas man is placed closer to Intellect, and is in touch with higher realities. Man is the intellectual principle, woman the sensual principle.

This idea has been detected in documents which are mainly of a religious and philosophical kind, and it constitutes an image, or picture of the male/female relationship as it was imagined. Whether the image of the feminine thus projected is also that of ordinary, popular thought, and whether it would have emerged in everyday conversation and attitudes, is entirely another question. It is most likely, however, that the Idea of Woman, as it emerges in the literature, is a construction which has its basis in instinctive, everyday thought: it should be regarded as a model which was used to constrain the behaviour of women, but which had already modified it to some extent, and had thus become social fact. The idea exists at a common level, which simply represents woman as sensuality, and man as mind. This notion can be seen from Philo, to Tertullian, to Muhammad. In it woman is simply the desire of the flesh, that which is immediately tempting; and that which is destructive of any permanency or strength of purpose: the passions are endless in variety, and so dissipate any single-minded intention. Man, on the other hand, has more of a natural focus on intellectual matters, and therefore on the first principles of the universe.

Plotinus' view of *eros* probably provides a key to the tragedy of Sophia, although of course he is building on Plato's Symposium. The discussion of love in *Ennead* III.5 (50) is most revealing on the general issues of passion, unrequited longing, and the determination of limits on emotions, all themes which were found to be intimately involved with the Valentinian portrait of Sophia. Love (*eros*) and desire (*orexis*) are distinguished in III.5 (50) 30, but the two are parallel faculties, the former applying itself to higher things, and the latter to lower things. They therefore function in a similar way, and Plotinus' characterisation of love casts light on his treatment of desire. Plato's *Symposium* myth is discussed, and the birth of Love from Poverty and Plenty. Love is defined as a state of being in perpetual need: it is in no way self-sufficient (III.5 (50) 5). The meaning of Love's symbolic parentage, from Poverty and Plenty, is scrutinised by Plotinus in order to discover how these origins are appropriate to Love. Plato's remark that Plenty 'was drunk with nectar since wine did not yet exist' is interpreted to mean that Love was born at an early stage in the generation of reality, when the physical world did not yet exist. Love was conceived therefore in the intelligible realm, and was made of form (*eidos*) and limitlessness (*aoristia*): this limitlessness was present because it had been a state of the soul prior to its knowledge of the Good. Therefore Love combines rationality with something 'limitless' and of 'obscure reality', and for this reason its results are defective, without self-sufficiency. Love has a 'limitless', 'irrational' and 'boundless' impulse (III.5 (50) 7). Then follows an important passage which speaks of Love's permanent incapacity for satisfaction, for Love 'will never be satisfied so long as he has within himself the nature of limitlessness'. It is recalled that Love is a mixture (*migma*) of a rational principle which did not stay within itself, but mingled with limitlessness. Love is therefore like a compulsion whose constant state is need: it has an inability to provide for itself given the two contrasting factors which make it a mixed phenomenon, one its nature as a rational principle (from this comes Love's ability to provide for itself), and secondly its nature as unlimited. It is the latter which guarantees that Love will be in a state of perpetual need, since Love is a thrust outwards which meets with no boundary to keep it checked within itself.

We have here an indication of what Horos means to Sophia, in the Valentinian myth. Sophia is in the state of suffering from these outward-directed passions until Horos (or Limit) is imposed upon her. In the myth this is presented as a stage in her salvation from the unsatisfied state. Like Love in Plotinus, she is suffering from lack of self-sufficiency, and from the impulsion outwards which comes with the passions, so that when a limit is encountered, the sense of lack is diminished. The imposition of a limit resolves the passions, and satisfies the lack (*endeia* in Plotinus). The Platonic understanding of *eros* must therefore be used to explicate the tragedy of the Valentinian Sophia, and this intimate blend of ideas does much to reveal how the image of the feminine is refined in a philosophical context. It is true that the notion of desire is one of the axes of Plotinus' philosophy; all things are said to be in a state of desire for the Good, which lacks nothing, is sufficient for itself, and provides measure and limit for everything (I.1 (53) 8), and this gives yet another glimpse into Sophia's plight. She is in a state of desire, since the ultimate principle, the Good, has not yet extended limit and measure to her, thereby providing her with a measure of self-sufficiency.

My suggestion is, then, that Sophia is a personification of aspects drawn from a Platonic notion of *eros*, some evidence of which we have from Plotinus. Sophia, or Desire, is all the more intense because it is bereft of substance, and is therefore in a certain sense parasitic. Passion is an impulsion away from oneself to the object of desire, which it seeks to obtain, and the living out of the desire is a state of pain, because it is the very realisation and assumption of the lack. To the mind belongs all the elements of form, measure, and intelligibility, to which the female aspires, but these are male properties. The figure of the androgyne reveals a belief that this radical polarisation of the image of the male and the female is disturbing, and that the beings thus envisaged are incomplete. Sexual individuation is revealed to be a predicament which can only be overcome by the recomposition of the sexes into one complete being.

Paul's writing reveals an interest in this same mode of thought, since in *Galatians* 3.28 he holds out the possibility of sexual divisions being transcended in some way. He seems to be talking about a state of being where such distinctions exist no more, but his fairly severely male-oriented prescriptions elsewhere in the New Testament show that he did not envisage social application of this principle. On the contrary, living within sexual distinctions (as well as class distinctions) was an inevitable consequence of living in society: thus women must keep silence in the churches, unless they are engaging in prophecy. The old Genesis principle of man having authority over the woman is also present in Paul's view of marriage, and in this respect Paul's thought constitutes a kind of re-statement of the traditional Jewish patriarchal concept of male/female relations, perhaps in reaction against a situation which was developing otherwise. It would be false, however, to claim that New Testament thought bypassed interest in social change, since it has a strongly ethical content which is aimed at influencing behaviour, but not at changing the structures within which this behaviour occurs.

The later Christian interpretation of Paul's annulment of the male/female distinction does not show any interest in its social application, but more in its consequences for the understanding of the metaphysical state which will be the result of Christian belief. An attempt to find annulment of sexual desire in accord with this verse resulted in the 'spiritual marriages' of male and female 'virgins' in late antiquity, and this is the extent to which Paul's verse may be said to have been socially applicable. The attempt to achieve asexuality resulted from a desire to hasten spiritual progress, and to reach the other-worldly ahead of time: it springs from an interest in what is called 'realised eschatology'. Side by side with this stood an attempt to retrace one's steps back through the Fall: the curse of *Genesis* was interpreted as applying to the lowest level of human life, and virginity in both males and females was advocated as an important stage in undoing the work of Adam and Eve.

However the thread which runs from Philo to the Koran is that which defines woman as sensuality. From the 'bashful virgins' laid up in paradise for the faithful Muslim, to the Alexandrian women denounced by Clement there is a clear identification of woman with the sexual element of life. As a result, control, reason and stability are regarded as male virtues, and as a further result man has been pictured as the master of woman in both the Islamic and Christian traditions.

General Index